HOW TO EMPOWER YOURSELF

AND GET MORE OUT OF LIFE

NEKITA PAUL

CITY HILL PRESS

Publish
Print
Design
Market

Print Edition

Publisher: City Hill Press

www.cityhillpress.com

CONTENTS

ACKNOWLEDGMENTS

While penning this work, I would get sudden bursts of thoughts along with sprightly energy, which I would quickly put down.

Firstly, I acknowledge El-Roi, the God who sees me and gave me the inspiration and message to impact his children worldwide.

My son Drew has been a sounding board and a source of joy even in my toughest days. I bless God for the privilege of parenting this king and world leader in the making.

I treasure my siblings Ifeyinwa Okafor, Vanessa Okonkwo, Ikenna Okafor, and Uchenna Okafor, who have been my support and sounding boards. I love you all.

I will not fail to mention some friends who have become sisters: Maureen Agu, Sylvia Ezeorji, Nneka Ene, and Ine Duke, who have provided me with both physical and emotional support in this journey called life.

I thank my publishing team and the gift that is Peculiar Medinus, who understood my vision and assignment and whose guidance and push cannot be understated.

I appreciate the long-standing friendships of Ade Shogbonyo, Lara Joel, and Uchenna Nnadi, who have been sources of strength.

To all the women out there who dare to believe they can break the norm and be counted.

To my late parents, Chief Dr Udoriri Okafor and Lolo Susan Nwanyinna Okafor, who instilled in me the belief that I could achieve anything and not be afraid to stand out from the crowd.

I love you always.

My Quotes

~

'Even if the world gives up on you, never ever give up on yourself.'

'Approach negativity with tunnel vision.'

- Nekita Paul

FOREWORD

Reclaim Your Potential with this Motivational Treasure.

The journey to conquering a lack of self-belief is a challenge many of us face, but now you can breathe a sigh of relief. *Nekita Paul* has developed a life-changing approach to personal growth and transformation in her motivational book, *Empower Yourself and Get More Out of Life*. This engaging and inspiring book has been meticulously developed with the goal of assisting individuals to unleash their utmost potential and achieve a more fulfilling life. With determination and effort, we can all strive to boost our health, relationships, careers, and various other aspects of our lives. *This captivating book unravels the significance of setting goals, formulating an action plan, and actively pursuing our dreams.*

Nekita dives deep into the perils of self-doubt and reveals how to overcome its shackles. Drawing from her journey of conquering personal struggle with self-belief, the author shares valuable insights and actionable steps that make this book truly stand out as a go-to guide for individuals wanting to empower themselves.

In a rapidly evolving world where gender roles continue to shift and expectations evolve, this book champions progress and encourages women to reclaim their place at the forefront of life. Rather than succumbing to self-imposed limitations, it is time to harness the power within and make the most of the precious gift of life.

From the dawn of time, women have often found themselves relegated to second-best, taking a backseat to their male counterparts. As the author noted, ancient creation stories are believed to be the source of gender power dynamics in which men took centre stage. Unfortunately, this narrative has negatively influenced women's self-perception for far too long, breeding limiting beliefs that hinder their true potential.

This groundbreaking book boldly traverses the complexities of a woman's mindset, sharing a personal journey into how these limiting beliefs have stifled women for decades. Simultaneously, it focuses on ways to challenge and alter this mindset, empowering women in the process.

Targeted at a general audience, this inspiring tome zeroes in on key aspects that resonate deeply with women. By stimulating self-discovery, goal-setting, and concerted action, it provides an indispensable roadmap to unlocking the power hidden within each of us.

Well-sourced principles and real-life experiences form the backbone of this masterful work. As someone who has battled and triumphed over a lack of self-belief, *the author* is a qualified and authentic voice on the subject. Equipped with a raw and honest account of her transformation, she offers readers the hope and encouragement needed to embark on their own self-improvement journey.

Empower Yourself and Get More Out of Life is packed with practical, easy-to-follow guidance that will have you captivated from the start. Key points emphasised in this motivational treasure include:

1. *Identifying the root causes of self-doubt:* Get to the core of your personal struggles and understand why you doubt

yourself in order to craft an effective self-improvement plan.

2. *Harnessing the power of positive thinking:* Adopt a mindset that cultivates resilience, self-assurance, and motivation.
3. *Developing actionable goals and strategies:* Learn the tools and techniques that turn aspirations into reality.
4. *Cultivating self-awareness and emotional intelligence:* Develop a deeper connection with yourself and others, fueling personal growth.
5. *Maintaining momentum and driving success:* Discover how to stay motivated and harness your newfound self-belief to achieve your goals.

This engaging guide passionately reminds readers that it is never too late to make pivotal changes and transform your life.

For those searching for a meaningful and impactful read, *Empower Yourself and Get More Out of Life* is the perfect companion. Packed with wisdom and practical guidance, it's a powerhouse of motivation that can help anyone conquer their self-doubt and achieve greatness. Begin your journey of self-improvement and embrace the version of yourself you've always yearned to be.

PECULIAR MEDINUS
Founder, Christian Sisters Network (CSN)
www.christiansistersnetwork.com

PREFACE

Life is an invaluable gift, brimming with countless opportunities for self-improvement and growth. While we all want to make the most of it, it is essential to challenge the limiting beliefs that may hold us back, especially for women, who have long been considered secondary to men. I've always wondered why society viewed women as inferior to men from the very beginning. It probably dates back to the story of creation, where men were created before women and have since seemingly come second in everything else. This book aims to inspire and guide you on a transformative journey to empower yourself and get more out of life.

Embarking on this journey begins with setting goals for yourself. It is crucial to have a clear vision of what you want to achieve. With your mind's eye, you can imagine it and have a clear picture of it in your mind, where all ideas start whether it involves your health, relationships, career, or any other aspect of life. By creating a roadmap to realising your goals, you can move towards building the life you desire.

Taking action is the next step in effecting positive change. Firstly, it's crucial to recognize the deeply rooted mindset and reality that have relegated women to a subordinate role for centuries, tracing back to creation myths where men emerged before women. Recognising this fact, which can also be a limiting belief, is the first step towards breaking free and pursuing our goals. The fact that a matter exists does not make it final; you can choose your own interpretation of that fact. Women being created second does not make them second; in fact, you may see them as an updated version of man, or, dare I say, a better version, more rounded.

This book will explore a woman's mindset and how a shift can empower her and set her up for greatness. It will highlight my personal journey in parts and how limiting beliefs have affected our species for decades, and try to change that mindset and empower ourselves in the process. It will conclude that by revealing the tools, strategies, and techniques to empower oneself, women can discover newfound confidence and resilience.

One of the most critical aspects of personal empowerment is taking care of your physical and mental well-being. This book explores different ways to prioritize self-care and cultivate healthy habits, leading to improved overall well-being.

Positivity breeds empowerment. Surrounding yourself with supportive and encouraging people can help you break free from limiting beliefs and create a nurturing environment for growth and success.

The ultimate purpose of this book is to uplift and inspire everyone, especially women facing limiting beliefs, by sharing powerful experiences, practical advice and tips. By embracing the journey of self-improvement and empowerment, we can all lead lives filled with meaning, passion, and achievements. And realise that we have God-given potential and talents to the maximum.

Join me on this transformative journey and learn how to break free from limiting beliefs, empower yourself, and get the most out of this incredible gift called life. Remember, it's never too late to make positive changes and create a better existence for ourselves. Let's thrive together! We can do this together! Yes, you can! I'm your number one fan!

1

____

UNLEASHING THE POWER OF SELF-BELIEF

Discover the transformative power of self-belief as the driving force that can propel you to greatness.

It all starts with belief in oneself and others (role models and authoritative figures like matriarchal and patriarchal personalities), who serve as sources of inspiration and encouragement. They can be a voice of steady support and direction. And who understands who you are and enables you to be the best version of yourself. This relates to the biblical reference in John 10:3-5. His sheep hear his voice and are led by him (paraphrased).

The journey of life beats that particular drum.. the seed, the roots.. the start is always belief... self-belief, especially as the propelling force that gets you from A to B, the bridge between the start and the finish. It's the fuel that makes you move. Think about it for a second. Every action you take in life starts with a "why." This driving force lies at the heart of your motivation and illuminates the reasons that propel you forward. Becoming aware of the reason behind your actions, as well as acknowledging and embracing the "why," will allow you to reconnect with your true self. Passion, fear, or the pursuit of a higher purpose can serve as the driving force behind every decision you make. By examining the "why" behind your actions, you can gain deeper insights into your motivations, aspirations, and personal values. Uncovering the "why" can empower you by inspiring self-belief, which has the potential to transform your life. This book will dive into the importance of understanding your reasons and embracing self-belief to propel you towards growth, success, and fulfilment.

Cultural Norms

In certain cultures, women are often raised with limiting beliefs due to the strong emphasis on the male child. As a result, their potential, dreams, and aspirations remain stifled, preventing them from harnessing their inner power. This process is termed conditioning. According to the Oxford Dictionary, it is the process of training or accustoming a person or animal to behave in a certain way or accept certain circumstances. Britannica defines conditioning as a behavioural process in physiology that increases the frequency or predictability of a response in a specific environment through reinforcement, typically in the form of a stimulus or reward for a desired response.

However, the time has come to challenge these beliefs and unleash the innate strength that every woman possesses. This chapter will discuss the transformative power of self-belief, empowering those confined by cultural norms to rise above them and chart their path to success. The impact of cultural conditioning on women's self-belief cannot be underestimated. In many societies, a deep-rooted belief in the superiority of the male child casts a shadow over the aspirations of countless women. It is essential to acknowledge that these cultural constraints have hindered the progress and potential of countless women across generations. Identifying this issue is the first step towards dismantling these restricting norms. These are parts of us; our inner voice may propel us on or hold us back. Our voice may be speaking out of fear, conditioning, or a lack of confidence, which are just a few reasons to doubt ourselves. Don't let that voice slow you down. Recognize those voices and subdue them. If you hear voices that say you can't do it, It can be your voice of self-doubt or probably the voices of people who don't believe in you (which you can hear in your head)—people who probably don't believe in themselves or anything and pass that on to you. Sometimes, negative voices can be indications that we are heading in the right direction. It may mean that we have taken giant strides that have attracted external doubt. We constantly have to be on guard against naysayers, both internal and external. What do we do with these negative voices? You ask to rattle the cage of negativity and replace it with the mind of Christ, as stated in Phil 4:8, which talks about replacing our thoughts with things that are true, noble, admirable, excellent and praiseworthy. (paraphrased).

Growing up as the second child of two educators, I was taught the importance of self-confidence early in life. My father, a university professor, and my mother, an educator and a nursery school proprietor, instilled in me a firm belief in my abilities. However, throughout my journey, naysayers and my own inner voice of self-doubt would often overshadow my self-belief. This often halted my progress and stifled my dreams before they could even begin. Then there is 'confidence', which is the enabler of self-belief.

There were times, even though I truly believed, I still lacked the competence and confidence to go ahead and achieve my goals. Needless to say, at that time, I made the wrong decisions for my path. You see, self-belief supports lofty ambitions, and you'll fly if you'll only believe it. The same is true for self-doubt, which will take you on a downward trajectory.

Despite my false starts, I found the strength to silence my negative voices. As I grew older, I began to realise I could control these voices and could eventually block them out. Gradually, I learnt to replace my self-doubt with uplifting thoughts and positive affirmations. Through persistence and determination, I raised my self-belief levels, realising my true potential. I set meaningful goals, developed self-awareness, and cultivated resilience. I learned that self-belief is a powerful driving force that can propel one to greatness. Through continuous learning and taking responsibility for my choices, I discovered the transformative power of self-belief.

However, I wasn't always this way, so like I mentioned earlier, my parents had instilled in me self-confidence and belief, which began to wane with my interactions at school and negativity being thrown and spoken at me. Whether it was my secondary school teacher who made negative comments like "You will never make a good lawyer because English is your second language," implying that I wouldn't be able to express myself effectively enough to succeed in such a career, Indeed, I started to internalize the negativity and began to question the initial belief my parents had instilled in me. I recall a time when I was much younger and on holidays from secondary school. I frequently participated in extracurricular activities and groups, such as Girl Guides and summer camps. I engaged in recreational cycling with other kids, engaging in friendly competitions as I traversed the local vicinity. On this particular occasion, I recall the sensation of complete liberation as I experienced the gentle breeze caressing my hair as I rode my bike, evoking a radiant smile upon my countenance. Then I would go ahead and race my friends down sidewalks with no care in the world, my self-belief and confidence in that activity at its full capacity.

As one matures and others speak about the dangers of bike riding, especially in the city, one begins to question the feasibility of riding or commuting by bicycle. A sense of scepticism arises, leading to self-doubt about riding and limitations. I hasten to add, despite the simplicity of this example, that the thought process is akin to a pool of water, composed of tiny drops. This is a tiny drop in the pool that adds up to self-doubt. At some point, I realised that this slow erosion of our self-belief and attitude can lead to an abyss of self-doubt and destruction. As I now stand before you, a testament to the power of self-belief, I urge you to always protect and nurture your own confidence. Remember, it is your responsibility to cultivate and strengthen your self-belief, never allowing it to wither away. With unwavering self-belief, there's nothing you cannot achieve.

Empowering myself and getting more out of life is my personal story and an ongoing journey of personal growth and self-discovery. I needed to strategize and apply mindset shifts that set me up for empowerment in order to make the most of my life. To achieve this, I used the following 10 steps:

Setting Meaningful Goals: By creating and aligning your long-term and short-term goals with your values and aspirations, these clear, well-defined goals will guide you on a purpose-driven journey, inspiring growth and success. This will serve as an atlas to guide you and keep you on your journey.

Develop Self-Awareness: By understanding and accepting your strengths, weaknesses, passions, and values, Self-awareness forms the foundation for living a life that is authentic and true to oneself. Getting to know yourself on a deeper level will allow you to make choices and decisions that are aligned with who you truly are and essentially develop and improve even more.

Cultivate a Growth Mindset: Believe in the potential to develop and improve your abilities through effort, dedication, and learning. Embrace challenges, and adopt a positive attitude towards failure as an opportunity to grow.

Embracing a growth mindset means believing that you can develop and improve your abilities through effort and learning. Seeing challenges as opportunities for growth and failures as valuable learning experiences allows you to build upon them. A powerful mindset shift empowers you to overcome obstacles and continuously strive for personal development. An example of this in my personal experience is dealing with difficult people. I worked as an event manager and had to deal with different clients and behaviours. In this example, I had a client who changed their mind at the last minute as to the colour scheme they wanted for their event. This gave me less time to source the materials and put me under a lot of pressure. Instead of reacting violently and cancelling the job, I engaged in a discussion with the client to understand the reason for the last-minute change, which turned out to be a tribute to her mom, who was travelling from overseas after initially facing visa denial. This reason, although sentimental and very important to the client, was not negotiable; therefore, my attitude toward her was to be as cooperative as possible within reason.

Practice Self-Compassion: In times of doubt or failure, treat yourself with kindness and understanding. This compassionate approach fosters resilience and personal growth. Accept that you are human and that making mistakes or facing setbacks is a natural part of life. Practice self-care, prioritise your well-being, and nurture a positive relationship with yourself.

Embrace Resilience: Life presents numerous challenges and setbacks. Cultivate the remarkable ability to bounce back from adversity, learning and growing stronger in the process. Develop coping mechanisms, stress management techniques, and a support network to help you navigate life's challenges. Resilience allows you to overcome setbacks and persevere in pursuing your goals.

Take Ownership of Your Choices: Recognise that you have the power within you to make choices that shape your destiny. Take responsibility for your decisions, actions, and outcomes. Remain true to your goals. Embrace a proactive mindset and focus on what you can control rather than dwelling on circumstances beyond your influence.

Building a Supportive Network: Surround yourself with supportive and uplifting individuals who inspire, encourage, and motivate you. Seek out mentors, friends, or communities that share your interests and values. Having a strong support network can provide guidance, encouragement, and accountability, helping you stay on track.

Continuous Learning: Never stop learning. Embrace personal growth and self-improvement as lifelong pursuits, continuously seeking to develop new skills and opportunities to expand your knowledge and broaden your perspective. Foster a mindset of growth and development. Stay curious, explore new ideas, and challenge yourself to step out of your comfort zone.

Practicing Gratitude: Cultivate an attitude of gratitude and appreciation for the present moment and the blessings in your life. Regularly reflect on the things you are grateful for, both big and small. Gratitude helps shift your focus towards positivity and abundance, enhancing your overall well-being.

Take Action: Transform your goals and dreams into reality by taking action. Your proactive approach will drive you closer to success, building your self-belief along the way.

Empowerment comes through action. Break your goals into actionable steps and consistently take small steps forward. Embrace the discomfort of uncertainty and take calculated risks. Progress and growth happen when you step out of your comfort zone and take action towards your aspirations.

Remember, empowering yourself is a lifelong journey. It is advisable to fully embrace the process, exercise patience with yourself, and then acknowledge and celebrate the progress achieved throughout the journey. By adopting these strategies and mindset shifts, you can empower yourself to live a more fulfilling and purposeful life. Every action has a reason that ultimately leads us to our true selves. By embracing the power of self-belief and understanding our motivations, we can unlock our fullest potential and lead a life of passion, growth, and success. So, why not dive deep into your "why" and empower yourself on this life-changing journey to self-discovery? Remember, self-belief is the ultimate catalyst for transformation.

KEY TAKEAWAYS:

- Never lose sight of your motivations and aspirations.

- Be wary of external and internal factors that can undermine self-belief.
- Use positive affirmations and thoughts to silence negative voices.
- Develop a growth mindset and practice self-compassion.

2

———

THE POWER OF AFFIRMATIONS

elcome to a pivotal chapter that introduces you to a potent tool that can improve your life: affirmations!

What are affirmations? Affirmations in New Thought and New Age terminology refer primarily to the practice of positive thinking and self-empowerment—fostering a belief that "a positive mental attitude supported by affirmations will achieve success in anything."

Affirmation is a powerful tool that can help you manifest your dreams and achieve your goals. Embrace the positive energy that comes with affirmations, and watch as they empower you to create the life you desire. Continue using affirmations to fuel your motivation, and embrace the power of affirmation—the act of declaring and confirming your truth.

Experience the empowering state of affirmation, where your potential is limitless. Believe in yourself and boldly claim something. Affirmation is a powerful declaration that confirms your truth and empowers you to achieve greatness.

Embrace the power of affirming and validating the truth or authenticity of your previous judgements, decisions, and similar matters. Affirmation empowers you to uplift and motivate yourself with positive words and impactful statements. The power of an affirmation lies in its ability to ignite both your conscious and unconscious minds, propelling you towards greatness.

It serves as a constant reminder of your limitless potential, fuelling your motivation and inspiring you to reach new heights in life. Embrace the transformative energy of affirmations and unlock the extraordinary within you.

It is normal for individuals to have moments of self-doubt and reflection on their lifestyle choices. However, it is important to remember that you have the power to overcome these negative thoughts and make positive changes in your life. Believe in yourself and embrace the journey towards a healthier and happier version of yourself.

You are capable of achieving greatness and living a life filled with positivity and self-acceptance. Keep pushing forward and never give up on your dreams. You have the strength within you to create the life you truly desire.

Affirmations, when embraced and spoken with conviction, have the power to ignite our inner fire and propel us towards greatness. They infuse our thoughts and actions with unwavering positivity, transforming our emotions, behaviours, and beliefs into unstoppable forces of success.

The power of affirmations knows no bounds! They have been the driving force behind countless individuals achieving amazing results all around the world. Furthermore, affirmations possess the incredible power to ignite positive change and empower you to transform your personal life.

Affirmations are powerful tools that ignite the fire within individuals, propelling them towards action and empowering them to achieve their wildest dreams. They serve as a guiding light, helping to sharpen focus and keep sight of the ultimate life goals. By harnessing the miraculous power of affirmations, negative thoughts are effortlessly transformed into positive ones, paving the way for a mindset shift and the adoption of a new, empowering belief system.

Embrace the potential of affirmations and unlock the limitless possibilities that await you! Most importantly, affirmations have the power to ignite positivity within you and pave the way for the revival or amplification of your self-confidence. They possess the power to empower us to achieve our life goals and reach a state of greatness.

To achieve remarkable results with affirmations, it is crucial to commit to reciting them daily with unwavering belief and whole-hearted enthusiasm. "I will focus on my own journey and embrace my unique qualities and strengths." This powerful affirmation is specifically crafted to ignite and amplify your self-confidence and self-worth.

To truly unlock the power of this statement, embrace its message wholeheartedly and make it a daily mantra. Remember, repetition is key! By affirming this uplifting message three to five times a day, you'll pave the way for positive transformation.

Let this motivational practice guide you towards greatness! Affir-mations are an incredibly powerful and life-changing tool that, when used wisely, empowers individuals to become unstoppable forces for positive transformation within their own spheres of influence.

Unleashing the Power of Positive Affirmations

Positive affirmations are not just motivational quotes or a feel-good fad. Researchers have found that repeating powerful positive phrases to oneself can rewire the brain and promote more constructive thought patterns. This helps in nurturing a growth mindset, combating negative self-talk, and promoting increased self-confidence.

Positive affirmations are highly effective instruments that will enable you to conquer harmful or pessimistic thoughts. You possess a remarkable capacity to utilise positive affirmations, stimulating your internal drive and facilitating personal growth, ultimately leading to enhanced self-confidence.

Affirmations, grounded in contemporary terminology, serve as a potent instrument for fostering a mental framework characterised by optimism and self-actualization. By adopting the conviction that maintaining a positive mental outlook, in conjunction with the practice of affirmations, can result in achievements throughout various spheres of existence, you will tap into your inherent capabilities and pave the way towards exceptional accomplishments.

Embrace the efficacy of affirmations and observe the transformation of your aspirations into tangible manifestations. Positive affirmations are highly effective instruments that have the potential to alter cognitive processes and enable you to foster a mental framework characterised by optimism and fortitude.

By intentionally choosing positive affirmations, you possess the capacity to restructure your cognitive processes and engender a significant transformation in your perception and engagement with the external environment. You should acknowledge the remarkable capacity inherent within you to influence your cognitive processes and affective experiences, thereby accessing an inexhaustible source of drive and happiness.

These affirmations possess a potent quality that can enhance your ability to maintain concentration on your objectives, eradicate any detrimental convictions, and recondition your subconscious mind to achieve success.

My three-step Programme for Effective use of Affirmations

Step 1:

Choose short and punchy affirmations (you don't have to recreate the will). Look up ones that speak to you online and appropriate them. That's what they are there for—to lift your spirit, energize you, and get you to action.

Step 2:

Put them up where you can see them daily. On your drawer or dressing table, your fridge is your screen saver.

. . .

Step 3:

Affirmations possess the capacity to inspire you to take action, enhance your focus on attaining life goals, facilitate the transformation of negative thought patterns into positive ones, and aid in the adoption of a new belief system. Most importantly, affirmations can yield significant benefits.

∼

Empirical research has demonstrated that neuroplasticity causes alterations to the brain, cellular structures, and genetic material through the persistent recurrence of specific thoughts. In essence, you can reconfigure specific cognitive patterns by employing positive affirmations. Positive affirmations are a self-help technique that involves the practical use of verbal statements.

People always wonder when to practice their affirmations. Are affirmations better practised at night or in the morning? Research findings suggest that the optimal period for practising affirmations is throughout the evening, specifically before going to sleep.

In the period preceding sleep time, our cognitive faculties enter a highly responsive state known as the theta state. This is the ideal moment to engage in the practice of positive affirmations for personal development, as they are more likely to be ingrained and result in desired outcomes in terms of mitigating insecurity, self-harm, and anxiety.

Recite the affirmation audibly for approximately five minutes, thrice daily, in the early hours of the day, noon, and night. It is ideal to engage in this practice while applying cosmetics or shaving since it allows individuals to observe their reflection in the mirror while reciting affirmative statements. This, in turn, gives you the energy you need for the day or the moment.

Affirmations have shaped me, and to date, I have carried on doing so. Whether it be words recited or from a favourite song, the result is usually the same: it connects and wakes up something within you and gives you that kick that sends a message to your brain. And here's what I think it tells your brain: Yes, you can do it! Whatever doubt, fear, or hesitation you may have had at that moment melts away like butter on a pan.

Research has indicated that the consistent use of positive affirmations has the capacity to restructure neural pathways within the brain. This implies that one has the capacity to profoundly alter the cognitive framework of their mind, typically within a relatively short span of a few weeks.

Consider the potential actions and emotional states that may arise from cultivating a more optimistic perspective. Through the practice of asserting positive affirmations about yourself, you will have the potential to alter your cognitive and emotional perceptions of yourself and your professional endeavours. This phenomenon has the potential to result in heightened self-assurance, enhanced productivity, and higher contentment in your professional trajectory. Positive affirmations have the potential to assist individuals in surmounting self-doubt and negative thought patterns.

In her scholarly discourse, psychologist Dr Lauren Alexander elucidates the potential benefits of incorporating daily positive affirmations into one's routine, positing that such practices can foster a sense of self-assurance and confidence in navigating the complexities of the external environment.

What is the psychology behind the affirmations you make? Here's the key: engaging in the activity stimulates the neural pathways and induces modifications in the brain regions associated with feelings of happiness and positivity. Multiple studies have also substantiated assertions that affirmations can lead to a reduction in stress levels that negatively impact health, an increase in individuals' engagement in physical exercise, and the adoption of healthier dietary habits such as eating greater quantities of fruits and vegetables, which can enhance academic performance.

Affirmations have the capacity to inspire individuals to take action, enhance their focus on attaining life goals, facilitate the transformation of negative thought patterns into positive ones, and aid in the adoption of a new belief system. Ultimately, affirmations hold significant potential.

Below are several examples of how you can incorporate self-belief and affirmations into your daily routine:

Positive self-talk

Empower yourself by focusing on your inner dialogue and replacing any feelings of insecurity or pessimism with uplifting affirmations. For example, if you find yourself thinking, "I lack sufficient ability," reframe it as "I possess ample competence and fully merit achievement." Engage in positive self-talk by consciously replacing negative or self-limiting thoughts with positive and empowering ones. For example, if you catch yourself thinking, "I can't do this," reframe it as "I am capable and have the skills to tackle this challenge."

Visualize

Embrace the power of visualization techniques to vividly imagine yourself triumphantly attaining your desired outcomes. Close your eyes and vividly imagine yourself succeeding, feeling confident, and enjoying the rewards of your efforts. This exercise is a powerful tool that strengthens your positive mindset and nurtures your unwavering self-belief. Take a few minutes each day to visualize yourself achieving your goals or engaging in activities that align with your aspirations. Imagine yourself confident, successful, and accomplished. Visualizing positive outcomes can reinforce self-belief.

Gratitude Journaling

Embrace the power of gratitude and uplift your spirits by jotting down at least three things you are truly grateful for every single day. This practice empowers you to embrace the positive aspects of your life, cultivating a deep sense of self-worth and gratitude.

Embrace the power of positivity and let it encompass you.

Surround yourself with powerful and uplifting individuals who wholeheartedly believe in your limitless potential. Engage in conversations and activities that uplift and inspire you. Limit exposure to negative influences that may undermine your self-belief.

Surround yourself with supportive and positive influences.

Spend time with individuals who believe in your abilities and encourage your growth. It is advisable to steer clear of relationships or environments that are toxic and have a detrimental effect on your self-confidence.

Set goals that are realistic and attainable.

It is advisable to decompose your overarching objectives into smaller, more feasible tasks. Attaining these incremental milestones can foster self-assurance and strengthen your belief in your abilities.

Celebrate your successes.

Acknowledge and celebrate your achievements, no matter how small. Recognize your progress, and give yourself credit for your efforts and accomplishments along the way. This reinforces your self-belief and motivates you to keep going. Celebrating small wins boosts confidence and reinforces a positive mindset.

Embrace the power of self-care.

Nurture your physical, mental, and emotional well-being with love and dedication. Embrace the empowering activities that fuel your spirit and invigorate your soul, such as engaging in invigorating exercise, finding inner peace through meditation, indulging in fulfilling hobbies, or immersing yourself in the awe-inspiring beauty of nature. When you make self-care a priority, you unlock your true potential and empower yourself to recognize your worth and value.

AFFIRMATION PRACTICE

Incorporate affirmations into your daily routine. Make a compilation of empowering affirmations that are congruent with your objectives and principles. Repeat these affirmations, either in the morning or before important tasks. Examples include: "I am deserving of success," "I have the courage to face any obstacles," or "I embrace my strengths and use them to achieve my goals.

Make positive affirmations regarding your personal attributes and capabilities, such as, "I am filled with confidence and unwavering belief in my abilities. I possess an incredible set of skills and knowledge that will undoubtedly lead me to success. I am capable of achieving anything I set my mind to." Say it with conviction, believing in their truth. By integrating these practices into your daily life, you can actively cultivate self-belief and reinforce positive affirmations. Over time, these habits can strengthen your mindset, boost your confidence, and help you overcome self-doubt.

Here are some concrete examples of how readers can practice self-belief and affirmations in everyday life:

Embrace the Power Within

Uncover and conquer the self-limiting beliefs that hinder your progress. Challenge yourself to question whether these beliefs are rooted in undeniable truths or merely unfounded assumptions or fears. Embrace challenges as opportunities for personal development and transformation. Stay focused on your goals and believe in your ability to overcome any obstacles that come your way. Remember, every setback is just a stepping stone towards your ultimate success. Keep pushing forward, stay determined, and never underestimate the power of your own potential. You have what it takes to achieve greatness, so embrace the journey and let your inner strength shine.

Engage in the practice of self-compassion by consistently treating yourself with kindness and understanding. Accept that making mistakes and facing setbacks are part of the growth process. It is advisable to give yourself the same level of empathy and compassion you would often give to a friend who is confronted with comparable difficulties.

Establish Realistic Goals

It is imperative to establish goals that are both clear and attainable while also pushing the boundaries of one's skills and fostering personal development. Breaking down bigger goals into smaller, actionable steps helps build momentum and confidence along the way.

Seek Feedback and Learning Opportunities

Embrace feedback as an opportunity for growth. Seek constructive criticism and learning opportunities to enhance your skills and knowledge. Embracing a growth mindset encourages continuous improvement and reinforces self-belief. These are just a few examples of how readers can apply the concepts of self-belief and affirmations in their daily lives. It's important to tailor these practices to individual preferences and needs. Regular practice and consistency will gradually strengthen self-belief and foster a positive mindset.

How to Embrace Independent Thinking with Affirmations

USE AFFIRMATIONS AS A TRANSFORMATIONAL TOOL

As noted earlier, affirmations are positive, powerful statements that, when repeated regularly, can rewire your thinking patterns and instil a greater sense of self-belief. By incorporating affirmations into your daily routine, you can replace your limiting beliefs with empowering thoughts and start cultivating independent thinking. As a transformational tool, affirmations reprogram the mind. Your thoughts form the foundation of your beliefs. By consistently reciting positive affirmations, you can rewire your brain to adopt a more optimistic and empowering mindset. This, in turn, has a significant impact on your actions, decisions, and overall well-being.

CREATE AND USE PERSONAL AFFIRMATIONS

To create a personal affirmation, start by picking a specific limiting belief you wish to overcome. Frame it in the positive and present tenses, as if you have already conquered it. For example, if your limiting belief is "I am not confident enough to speak up," your affirmation could be, "I am confident in expressing my thoughts and opinions."

Select three to five relevant affirmations and repeat them first thing in the morning, throughout the day, and before bed for best results. Over time, you will notice a significant shift in your mindset and self-confidence.

REINFORCE YOUR AFFIRMATIONS THROUGH ACTION

While affirmations are powerful on their own, combining them with action steps will expedite your journey to self-empowerment.

For instance, if your affirmation declares that you are a confident public speaker, sign up for a public speaking course or join a local Toastmasters group. By aligning your beliefs and actions, you create a more robust foundation for lasting change.

SEEK SUPPORT AND SHARE YOUR PROGRESS

It can be helpful to find a like-minded community that understands the power of affirmations and encourages growth. Share your progress, challenges, and triumphs with people who are on a similar journey of self-improvement. By surrounding yourself with positive energy and support, your path to empowerment will be smoother and more enjoyable.

The Power of Positive Affirmations for Women

Each day, we go through countless mental and emotional challenges. Women often face societal pressures and limiting beliefs that dampen their confidence and lower their expectations of what they can achieve. We will delve into the amazing potential of positive affirmations to transform the way a woman views herself and unlock limitless potential. Thankfully, with the help of positive affirmations, a woman can combat these limiting beliefs and reignite the flame of self-love, self-confidence, and resilience.

Let's explore the key points that make positive affirmations a game-changing tool for personal growth for women:

Boosting Self-Esteem and Self-Worth

Positive affirmations challenge the pervasive, harmful ideas that women should be submissive or inferior. By replacing these thoughts with statements that emphasise self-worth, women begin to truly recognise their value and innate capabilities.

Positive affirmations help reinforce a woman's self-worth and heal her relationship with herself, taking her from a place of doubt and fear to one of self-love and compassion.

Reducing Anxiety and Stress

Studies have shown that positive affirmations can lower stress hormone levels, allowing for improved emotional regulation and stress management. This is especially beneficial for women, who juggle multiple personal and professional roles.

Achieving Goals and Creating Lasting Change

Positive affirmations provide a mental scaffold for success. Women who use affirmations as part of their daily routine are more likely to set and achieve ambitious goals, as they internalise the belief that they are capable and deserving.

Overcoming Limiting Beliefs and Breaking Stereotypes

A continuous stream of positive affirmations enables women to outgrow the limiting beliefs that may have been ingrained since childhood.

By countering stereotypes and elevating one's self-image, women can break free from the societal barriers that often hold them back.

Inspiring Joy and a Positive Outlook on Life

An overall sense of happiness and fulfilment blossoms as women begin to practice positive affirmations and witness their effect on everyday life.

Ditching negative self-talk in favour of empowering statements allows for a brighter, more optimistic outlook on life.

Enhancing Intuition and Decision Making

An empowered mindset enhances your ability to trust your intuition and make bold choices that align with your goals, leading to greater fulfilment and a newfound sense of control in life.

Embark on Your Journey of Positive Affirmations and Transform Your Life

To take your personal growth journey to the next level and harness the power of positive affirmations, consider making them a non-negotiable part of your daily life. Regular practice and consistency are keys to unlocking their full potential.

Create a customised list of affirmations that resonate with your personal values and aspirations, then carve out dedicated time each day to repeat them while fully internalising their meaning.

How to Incorporate Positive Affirmations into Your Daily Life

Begin your journey with these three simple yet effective steps:

1. **Start from the heart:** Reflect on your limiting beliefs and which areas of your life need the most attention. Craft personalised affirmations that address those concerns.
2. **Repetition is key:** Consistently recite your affirmations, ideally out loud, every day, preferably morning and night, to set the tone for your day and prepare for restorative sleep.
3. **Practice mindfulness:** As you repeat your affirmations, focus on the emotions and sensations they evoke.

Embrace those emotions and visualise yourself embodying the affirmations completely.

Examples of Powerful Positive Affirmations for Women

To get started, here are five empowering affirmations to inspire you:

1. I am strong, capable, and resilient.
2. I deserve love, respect, and happiness.
3. I release the need for approval from others and trust my own intuition.
4. I am enough, just as I am.
5. I am worthy of success, abundance, and contentment.
6. I see failure as a golden opportunity to learn.
7. I know that massive action cures everything.
8. I love the creative energy that flows through me.
9. I work for my desires because I don't want regret.
10. I don't live for things; I live for a spiritual purpose.

Key Points:

The chapter delved into the importance of affirmations for breaking down limiting beliefs and empowering women to become independent thinkers. The chapter showcased strong points as to why positive affirmations should be an essential part of every woman's daily routine. Some of the key points include:

1. The psychological effects of positive affirmations lie in your ability to counteract negative self-talk, which can be deeply ingrained and limiting in nature.
2. An array of practical ways to incorporate affirmations into everyday life are presented to offer you multiple avenues to implement changes in your thinking processes.

3. An essential aspect of adopting affirmations is to genuinely believe in your capability to create and maintain lasting change.
4. The chapter showcased inspiring examples of individual journeys and personal transformations attributed to the use of daily affirmations.

I believe that this chapter about affirmations holds immense potential to inspire and usher in transformative changes in your life. Affirmations are an invaluable instrument in this journey towards independent thinking and self-empowerment.

By recognising your limiting beliefs, harnessing the power of affirmations, taking action, and seeking support from others, you'll pave the way to a life with more freedom and fulfilment. Integrating positive affirmations into your daily routine is an essential step towards achieving female empowerment and personal growth.

By doing so, women will break through limiting beliefs, experience increased self-worth, and lay the foundation for transformational change in all aspects of their lives. The journey towards personal empowerment starts with a single step, and that step is now.

Utilise the power of positive affirmations to unleash your true potential and transform your life from within, one empowering statement at a time. Embrace this practice, and watch as your life unfolds into a masterpiece of confidence, self-love, and undeniable inner strength.

Group Exercise

In groups, discuss how integrating affirmations into your life has transformed your life, or how their use has fostered a sense of community and support.

Consider how your situation has improved or deteriorated since you began utilizing them.

3

WHO AM I?

YOU DETERMINE THAT!

That's a great question, to which I would give this great answer. You are who you want to be. You hold the key to your world; all you need to do is use it.

I sometimes imagine a world where you never have stress, challenges, sadness, or pain, and I wonder if I will know how to appreciate a book like this. How will I know gratitude? Only a song, an insane shout, a crazy dance, or tears can convey that feeling. How will I know how to pull someone into an embrace so tight as to squeeze some life juice into myself and quench the thirst that only skin can fill?

I'm grateful for my struggles. God has carefully placed them in my life so that I can build character. The character that will qualify me to give to the world all the precious gifts He put inside me to give to you. The obstacles I've faced are no coincidence. They were intentional. Embrace your struggles, and you will get to the mountaintop to caress the underbelly of the clouds.

If the mountain was smooth, you possibly couldn't get to the top.

It took me a while to understand this principle. I always asked, Why me? Why did it always have to happen when it was my turn? Why didn't my relationship turn out to be beautiful? Why did my promotion have to take twice as long as my peers? Why do I feel that life has been unfair to me all the time? The questions were endless.

So, I stopped asking myself those questions and instead focused on what I could learn from those situations, realizing that I still had to live through them. Why not take a lesson from them and regain control? I gradually regained my sense of powerlessness as I delved into the lesson underlying the problem.

I began to see objectively where I went wrong. The attitude behind the issues I was facing was usually wrong and also firmly in my control. It was indeed something I could change, given that it was in my gift to do so. Thus, I started building character. My very behaviour began to change; words that could hardly be used to describe me before were now being used. 'Nekita, you are so patient' and 'You listened to my version of events till the end' signalled that a change had taken place and it was manifesting in the physical world. I was metamorphosing into the butterfly I always aspired to be deep down. I always wanted to be the best version of myself, and alas, that was finally happening. I could see the horizon far away. I certainly had more to go, but hey! I was happy that change had crept in and I was on my way to my best self.

As a child prodigy, Tiger Woods received coaching and mentorship from his late father, Els Wood. He had a meteoric rise and then had personal challenges that led to his crash, coupled with a series of back injuries and surgeries. He was completely written off. No one believed he would ever come back to play top golf, never mind win a major. What a remarkable comeback from him! It was his belief in himself that, no matter what life threw at him, his singular belief in himself and tunnel vision in that regard enabled him to come back even better.

The key lesson is to focus on yourself and your goal, drown out the noise, and literally rise above the naysayers and haters. That's the image I envision when I engage in the mental exercise of erasing negativity. This helps me to actually feel myself making that upward movement. (Try it once in a while.) I'm positive it will do you good.

Tunnel Vision Concept

Seeing things only in front of you and not considering other factors that you may not see—I call it tunnel vision. According to doctors at my.clevelandclinic.org Tunnel vision is another name for peripheral vision loss. It makes it hard or impossible to see objects that aren't directly in front of you. It can be temporary, but it might also permanently change your vision, depending on what causes it.

However, for the purpose of this book, tunnel vision is when one focuses on a single goal or point of view and can't see the bigger picture or the greater advantages. This, in turn, limits their worldview and understanding of life's lessons, or the learning experience that presents itself in front of them.

One such scenario comes to mind. Imagine hitting that goal without being hindered by what comes at you. The picture that comes to mind is of you playing baseball while standing at the spot. You have just pitched and dropped the bat to score a run. At that moment, you are focused on getting home without the ball being caught or stopped by your opponent. You are so focused on your run that you don't see the crowd cheering you on, but you don't see the opponent running for the ball. You just keep going forward, although you know these things are happening around you. You've managed to drown out the stadium's noise, which is full of people cheering you on. You remain undeterred and determined, staying on course, and alas, you score! hurray!

DISCOVERING YOUR WORTH:
EMBRACING THE CREATION THAT YOU ARE

Have you ever asked yourself, "Who am I?" It's a question everyone faces at some point in their lives, and the answer determines your value and your sense of self. For me, the answer lies in the Bible, which is a source of strength for me. The power to define your identity and worth lies within you, and the starting point for this inner exploration is acknowledging the profound love of your Creator.

"You are fearfully and wonderfully made (Psalm 139:14)."

The foundation of your personal journey begins with these words from your Creator: "You are fearfully and wonderfully made." This profound declaration emphasises the love, care, and thoughtfulness that were invested in your creation. Your journey to self-discovery starts with accepting this truth and holding onto it as a constant reminder of your unique worth and importance in this world.

Take a Cue!

In a world dominated by male dominance, the Bible tells the story of Esther, a Jewish queen, who used her inner power of self-discovery to carve out her own identity. Just like Esther, you have the power and choice to define who you are and what you stand for. Deep within her, she understood her Creator's love, and this propelled her to the frontlines, fighting tirelessly for the victory of her people.

As you dive into this inspiring story, imagine the immense courage and self-awareness it took for Esther to approach the king without a formal invitation, knowing the potential consequences of doing so. However, she remained unwavering in her faith, armed with the belief that her God could bring victory to her people.

This tale has a significant lesson for women everywhere: the power to determine your identity lies in your own hands. Embrace the true essence of who you are, and let that guide you through life's challenges. Just as Esther did, stand tall and face the world head-on, claiming your own victories and ensuring that no one else dictates your path.

In our lives, it is essential to recognise who we are and to draw strength from this knowledge. Remember, your Creator's love and support are unyielding, just as they were for Esther. Rely on this truth to overcome boundaries and prejudices and become the person you were always meant to be.

Through the story of Esther, a resolute Jewish Queen, we can all learn the incredible power of self-discovery and the unwavering conviction in our Creator's support. Delve into your own journey of self-discovery, envision your victory, and take charge of your destiny.

BREAKING FREE:

OWNING YOUR IDENTITY AND REDEFINING CULTURAL EXPECTATIONS

As you grow up, you might be overwhelmed by the cultural norms and expectations placed on women. However, it's time to break free and take charge, for the only person who defines **you** is **yourself**. This chapter will explore the power of self-determination, debunk the myths surrounding cultural expectations, and empower you to challenge the status quo. Remember, you have the ultimate control over your identity and how you choose to navigate the world.

Having said that, let's move forward to understanding the struggle of assimilating into the traditional norms of society.

Challenging the Cultural Narrative

The cultural narrative on the treatment of women often revolves around antiquated expectations, from appropriate behaviour and attire to predetermined roles within the family and society. It is no secret that these rules can be restrictive and stifling, and you are not alone in questioning their merit and relevance in today's world.

It is important to recognise that your inner sense of self and worth are not solely defined by external factors or societal approval. Embrace your unique qualities and challenge norms that don't align with your values. Remember, you determine who you are.

Self-Discovery and Redefining Personal Values

The process of self-discovery typically involves learning about one's desires, interests, and beliefs. It requires honest self-reflection, experimentation, and open-mindedness. As you embark on this journey, don't be afraid to venture outside of the traditional cultural expectations or even to push those boundaries.

Through self-discovery, you will not only redefine your personal values but will also cultivate confidence and resilience. Remember that this journey is about finding out who you truly are as well as establishing your identity.

Supporting and Learning from Other Women

Supporting and learning from other women who have also questioned and defied cultural norms can be incredibly empowering. Surround yourself with these inspiring role models and foster connections with like-minded individuals. By doing so, you create a network of supportive, understanding, and empowering allies on your journey to self-discovery and asserting your identity.

The Power of Choice

Ultimately, the power of choice resides in your hands. Consider the social constructs that have shaped your understanding of what it means to be a woman, and decide which ones resonate with your beliefs and values. It is essential to remember that the definition and image of an ideal woman are ever-evolving, just like you.

As you progress through this chapter and continue your path to self-discovery and embracing your identity, bear in mind that there is no one-size-fits-all solution to challenging cultural norms. Each person's journey is unique, and it is vital to honour your own truth and embrace your authentic self. With courage and confidence, own your identity and redefine the expectations placed on you by society. You possess the power to create a path that aligns with your values and purpose, and in doing so, inspire other women to do the same.

Harnessing the Power of Your Past

Think back to a time when you felt truly empowered, appreciated, or loved. Close your eyes and imagine the scene, the people involved, and the emotions you experienced. Can you recall the sensation of euphoria and confidence that washed over you? These powerful memories can be used as a catalyst on your journey of self-discovery, allowing you to explore the depths of your identity and uncover your true potential.

Up to You!

Accept the challenge of self-exploration by asking yourself this seemingly straightforward question: Who am I? As you embark on this journey, you'll come to realise that you, and only you, have the power to define yourself. By leveraging your unique experiences and capabilities, you'll find your voice and create your own narrative. And as you delve deeper, you'll start to understand your strengths, weaknesses, passions, fears, and dreams.

Reflect on Empowering Experiences

The first step in this introspective adventure is to revisit your most empowering moments. Consider the instances when you accomplished something significant, faced your fears, or were recognised for your hard work. Reflect on the qualities you displayed in those situations and how they contributed to your triumph.

Dig deep into your past to identify memories where you felt capable, strong, and self-assured. Such moments often reveal the confident, determined, and resourceful individual you truly are. By examining these experiences, you can start consciously building the version of yourself that you aspire to become.

Cherish Moments of Appreciation and Love

Next, look back on the times you felt appreciated or loved by others. These positive emotions are instrumental in the formation of strong relationships, fostering connections with others, and maintaining a sense of belonging. Recognising moments of genuine support can help you understand your value and reinforce your self-worth.

Remind yourself that appreciation and affection aren't solely dependent on external validation. It's essential to appreciate and love yourself just as much. Nurture yourself by treating your body with kindness, respecting your limits, and indulging in activities that bring you joy and relaxation.

Embracing Change and Growth

Allow yourself to change, evolve, and grow as a result of your self-discovery voyage. As you uncover different aspects of yourself, acknowledge that your identity may not be static; people change and evolve over time. It's a natural part of life's journey.

Embrace personal growth by taking risks, trying new experiences, and challenging yourself. This proactive approach will unveil aspects of yourself that might have been dormant, awaiting awakening.

The journey of self-discovery can be a long-lasting, transformative process. As you leverage your memories of empowerment, appreciation, and love, you'll uncover your true sense of identity and unlock your fullest potential. Always remember that you alone have the power to determine who you are, so why not embark on this adventure and unveil the marvellous, authentic you?

Embrace the Journey:
Quotes on Self-Discovery for Women

Are you ready to embark on a journey of self-discovery? Whether you're feeling lost or searching for inspiration, these quotes will empower you to find your path. As a woman, sometimes it's hard to decide what direction to navigate through our ever-changing lives. Regardless of your age, there will always be room for growth, self-improvement, and transformation. After all, it's up to *you* to determine who you are! So, buckle up and let these powerful words stay with you as you set forth.

"The only person who defines you is you. The journey of self-discovery begins with the act of deciding what it means to be oneself." - Oprah Winfrey
Oprah reminds us that the power to define ourselves lies in our own hands. Start by asking yourself, "Who am I?" Your answer should come from within, not from what others dictate.

"I can be changed by what happens to me. But I refuse to be reduced by it." - Maya Angelou
Maya's words teach us that life experiences can shape us, but we have the power to rise above those challenges. Embrace the lessons and keep moving forward.

"To be yourself in a world that is constantly trying to make you something else is the greatest accomplishment." - Ralph Waldo Emerson
This Ralph Waldo Emerson quote highlights the importance of embracing our individuality. Don't let societal pressures influence you; instead, celebrate your uniqueness.

"One's life has value so long as one attributes value to the life of others, by means of love, friendship, and compassion." - Simone de Beauvoir
Philosopher Simone de Beauvoir reminds us that our lives' value is linked to how we treat others. Nourishing our relationships and showing compassion are essential for personal growth.

"The most courageous act is still to think for yourself. Aloud." - Coco Chanel
Coco Chanel's bold statement emphasises the importance of not just

forming our own opinions but also expressing them with confidence.

"Remember always that you not only have the right to be an individual, you have an obligation to be one." - Eleanor Roosevelt
Eleanor Roosevelt encourages us to not only embrace our individuality but also to ensure it enriches the world around us. It's our duty to be the best versions of ourselves.

As you ponder these powerful quotes, let the words serve as a guiding light for your journey of self-discovery. Remember that the key to unlocking your potential lies within you. So, embrace your uniqueness, spread love and kindness, and always stay true to who you are. After all, *you* are the one who determines your identity.

Throughout this chapter, we have discussed numerous ways to understand and discover your inner self. By truly engaging with these concepts, you will be on a path towards a more authentic and fulfilling life. Remember, you hold the keys to uncovering your true self, and with time and dedication, you will create the life you deserve.

Lean on the insights shared in this chapter, be open to the journey, and arm yourself with courage as you delve into the mysterious and profound realm of self-discovery. So, go ahead and celebrate the person or woman that you are; boldly embark on this enlightening adventure; and take a fearless step towards defining your own narrative.

As you continue to move forward, don't forget to pause, reflect, journal, and appreciate the progress you make. Your journey of self-discovery may be challenging at times, but the rewards of knowing and embracing your authentic self will be unparalleled. Remember, you have the power, wisdom, and strength to shape your destiny and unveil your true identity. The only limits are the ones you place on yourself.

4

———

START WHERE YOU ARE

HERE AND NOW!

The brand slogan of the renowned shoe company, Nike, has always resonated with me. "Just do it!" I have always liked this saying, although I have not always followed through with action.

I don't know about you, but there was a time in my life (not so long ago) when I would give myself every excuse in the book in order not to do my scheduled work. I would prioritize the smaller tasks over the larger ones, which required more attention and were of higher priority, resulting in a lack of completion within the allotted time. Perhaps it was my inner fear of hard work, or the fact that it would take longer to see results, that led me to self-sabotage and opt for quick-win tasks that would yield results sooner.

Have there been times in your life when you have self-sabotaged in this way?

Have you followed through on a course of action without procrastinating?

Work can be defined as a task or tasks to be undertaken that involve mental or physical effort to achieve a purpose or result. We all have to work to achieve results. Usually, there is a sequence that must be followed to achieve the desired outcome.

I have learned that planning and managing our expectations

while we work is something that will help motivate us.

If you're feeling motivated and ready to make a start, here are some practical steps you can take:

Overcome Procrastination

It's time for you to break free from procrastination. You might have grown up in an environment that constantly told you that you couldn't do something or anything, for that matter, but that doesn't mean it's true. This chapter will show you how to take the first steps towards conquering procrastination and unleashing your true potential.

You might have heard phrases like *"you're not good enough"* or *"you'll never succeed"* from the people around you, and you have internalised them as part of your identity. Take a moment to remember that these beliefs are not based on facts or your true identity; they are merely the opinions and judgments of others who may not be equipped with all the facts of your story, let alone come to those conclusions. It's time for you to challenge and rewrite those words and beliefs with more empowering ones that serve and uplift you.

To conquer procrastination, you need to start by understanding why you procrastinate in the first place. Perhaps your procrastination stems from fear—fear of failure, fear of judgment, or fear of not being perfect. But the truth is, no one is perfect, and everyone experiences failure at some point. What matters is how you learn from those experiences and use them as stepping stones to grow and succeed. The first steps against procrastination are listed below:

1. **Set Clear Goals:** Clearly articulate what you want to achieve with this move. It could be related to your career, education, relationships, or personal development. Having a clear goal will help guide your decision-making process.
2. **Break Defined Goals into Smaller Tasks** - Having a clear picture of what you want to achieve and breaking it down

into smaller, manageable tasks will make it less overwhelming and easier to handle.

3. **Gather information:** Conduct research and gather as much relevant information as possible about the move you want to make. This could include researching job opportunities, educational programmes, or locations you're considering. The more informed you are, the better equipped you'll be to make an informed decision.

4. **Assess the risks and benefits:** Consider the potential risks and benefits associated with the move. Evaluate the potential challenges you might face and determine if the potential rewards outweigh them. This assessment will help you weigh your options and make an informed decision.

5. **Prioritize your tasks** - Determine the most important and urgent tasks at hand and start working on them. This will help you make progress and experience a sense of accomplishment, which fuels motivation.

6. **Create a schedule** - Allocate a specific time slot for each task and stick to it. This helps to create structure and discipline, making it harder for you to procrastinate. Develop a detailed plan of action. Set timelines, identify resources you may need, and establish milestones along the way. A well-structured plan will help you stay organised and focused on your goal.

7. **Take action:** Once you have your plan in place, start taking action. Begin by tackling the smaller tasks, and gradually work your way towards the larger ones. Be proactive and persistent in pursuing your goal.

8. **Adapt and adjust:** Understand that plans may change along the journey. Be open to adjusting your approach as needed, based on new information or unforeseen circumstances. Flexibility and adaptability are key when making a move.

9. **Seek support** - Don't be afraid to ask for help or to share your goals with friends, family, or mentors. They can provide valuable encouragement, advice, and accountability.

10. **Eliminate distractions** - Identify and eliminate distractions that get in the way of your productivity. This might mean turning off your phone, closing unnecessary tabs on your computer, or finding a quiet working space.

11. **Believe in yourself and celebrate your achievements** - Remember to appreciate your accomplishments, no matter how small they may seem. You're capable of achieving incredible things, and acknowledging your achievements will help reinforce this belief.

12. **Practice self-compassion** - Be gentle with yourself when things don't go as planned or if you fail at something. Recognise that you're only human, and use each setback as an opportunity for growth.

13. **Stay motivated and persistent:** Making a move can be challenging, and you may encounter obstacles or setbacks. Stay motivated by reminding yourself of your goal and the reasons why you want to make this move. Surround yourself with positive influences, and seek support when needed. Persistence and determination will help you overcome hurdles and stay on track.

Remember, the specific steps you need to take will depend on the nature of the move you're making. Tailor these general guidelines to your specific situation, and trust yourself to make the best decision for your own personal growth and happiness.

By implementing these strategies and actively challenging your limitations and limiting beliefs, you're paving the way to a more fulfilling, productive, and empowered life. Remember, the power to change your narrative and overcome procrastination lies within you. It's time for you to believe in yourself and unlock your true potential.

Like a treasure buried deep down, there is greatness within you! Go forth, conquer, and thrive!

Recognise and Overcome Personal Sabotage

Do you ever find yourself standing in your way? Are your self-doubts and inhibiting beliefs holding you back from living your best life? If so, you're not alone. Many women struggle to understand when they're self-sabotaging and breaking free from these destructive patterns. It could be the result of years of being put down or told 'you can't do it' that finally rang true. Whatever the case, it's in your gift to either receive or block negative, belittling, or limiting beliefs.

Identifying When You're Sabotaging Yourself

The first step to overcoming self-sabotage is recognising when you're doing it. You may experience self-sabotage in various aspects of life, such as your career, personal relationships, or even your self-esteem. Here are some common ways personal sabotage shows itself:

- **Perfectionism:** Setting impossibly high standards for yourself can be paralysing or result in burnout.
- **Negative self-talk:** Constantly belittling or undermining yourself through your thoughts and inner dialogue
- **Fear of failure or success:** Avoid taking risks or pursuing opportunities out of fear of failure or fear of succeeding.
- **People-pleasing:** Neglecting your own needs or boundaries in order to win approval or avoid conflict with others.
- **Confessing the wrong notion of one's self:** believing the rhetoric and lies being spewed about you by naysayers.

Strategies to Overcome Self-Sabotaging Behaviours
Now that you can identify the patterns of personal sabotage, it's

time to build strategies to overcome them. Here's how to work on dismantling your limiting beliefs and embracing a more empowering mindset:

1. **Awareness:** Develop a conscious awareness of your self-sabotaging thoughts and actions by journaling, meditating, or openly discussing them with a trusted friend or therapist.
2. **Be Kind to Yourself:** Eradicating negative self-talk starts with treating yourself with kindness, understanding, and empathy. Speak to yourself as you would speak to a dear friend.
3. **Develop realistic objectives:** Establish achievable and specific objectives for yourself, and create a clear plan of action to reach those goals.
4. **Embrace imperfection:** Let go of the idea of perfection and give yourself permission to make mistakes. Remember, you can still learn from your successes and failures.
5. **Build a support network: Surround yourself with people who encourage and empower you, as well as those who challenge you to grow and break free from your limiting beliefs.**
6. **Practice self-care:** Prioritise your emotional, mental, and physical well-being by engaging in activities that bring you joy, relaxation, and balance.
7. **Acknowledge your progress:** Celebrate both your small victories and major milestones. Recognise that growth and change are continuous processes, and every step counts.
8. **Speak positive thoughts out loud which in turn reinforces the belief**

Recognising and overcoming personal sabotage is crucial for women who strive to break free from limiting beliefs and unlock their full potential. Developing awareness, cultivating self-compassion, and taking intentional actions to change destructive patterns will significantly increase your chances of success. Empower yourself today by making a conscious effort to identify and overcome any self-sabotaging behaviours you might have and taking a decisive step towards living your best life.

Reflections:

It's time to reflect, discover the deep-seated truth of your sabotage, and realise that you have what it takes to overcome it.

Revisit the Root of Your Self-Sabotage

Look within you and understand the limiting beliefs that might be causing you to self-sabotage. Do you often feel like you're not good enough, or that you don't deserve success or happiness? These inner thoughts can become significant barriers, preventing you from reaching your goals. Take a moment to reflect on what might be holding you back; write these beliefs down, and then challenge them with evidence from your achievements and capabilities.

Embrace Your Strengths

Focus on your strengths! Make a list of your positive attributes, skills, and accomplishments. By honing in on your strengths, you will start to build confidence and shift the repeated pattern of self-sabotage.

Where is your self-worth when compared to your values?

To overcome self-sabotage, it's crucial to be realistic about this: Your self-worth and your values! Does your daily objective align with your values, priorities, and passion? Do you give away your time instead of focusing on the present and what you can achieve right now?

Where are Your Positive Influences?

Are those who uplift, inspire, and support you, friends, family members, or mentors? Do you have a strong support system that can help you stay motivated and encouraged, even when you feel like giving up? Do you actively seek out positive influences or hesitate to ask for their advice when you need it?

Practice Mindfulness

Focus on incorporating mindfulness into your daily routine. By practicing mindfulness, you can become more aware of your thoughts and emotions, which will help you identify potential cases of self-sabotage before they take hold. Additionally, treat yourself with kindness and understanding, as you would someone you love.

Conquer self-sabotage by starting where you are right now and embracing your worth. By applying these strategies, you'll gain the skills and mindset necessary to overcome limiting beliefs and unlock your full potential. Remember, you are a strong, capable, and fierce woman, and it's time to step into your greatness and let your true self shine!

Develop a Degree of Autonomy

It's time to *rethink* your dependence on others, particularly on men, for even the simplest of tasks. Maybe you find yourself holding back due to fear, insecurity, or just feeling overwhelmed. You don't need to rely on anyone else when you have the strength and power within you!

Firstly, just analyse the idea that you always need others, namely men, to handle even the most basic of tasks. This belief might stem from stereotypes or societal norms, but it's simply not true. It has been proven time and time again that women are just as capable of accomplishing great things, both big and small.

Keys to Note:

- **You have the power within you:** You possess incredible strength and resilience. Whatever it is you're seeking help with, there's a high chance you can do it yourself! Don't sell yourself short; trust in your abilities and take charge of the task at hand.
- **Challenging limiting beliefs:** Don't be held back by notions of what you *should* or *shouldn't* do based on others' opinions or expectations. With God's help, you are more than capable of determining what's best for you.
- **Take small steps:** Overwhelming yourself with lofty goals or tasks can be daunting. Break down your challenges into smaller, more manageable pieces, and enjoy the satisfaction of conquering them one by one. Before you know it, you'll have broadened your horizons and grown beyond your previous limitations.
- **Embrace the learning process:** Even if you're a beginner at something, it's never too late to start learning and growing. Accept that mistakes will happen and be gentle with yourself; after all, nobody's perfect! So go ahead and embrace the journey, knowing that you're only going to get better and smarter with every passing day.
- **Blow your own trumpet**- sing your own song ,only you know yourself best.

So, it's time to ditch those limiting beliefs and take the world by storm! Remember, the key to success is already within you. Trust God, but believe in yourself and start where you are, right here and now! Let's make the most of this incredible journey we call life and embrace the boundless opportunities that lie ahead!

As you reach the conclusion of this empowering chapter,

remember that it's never too late to start making changes to better your life.

By now, you should have a better understanding of how to overcome procrastination and seize the present moment. It's crucial to recognise that delays and putting things off can significantly hinder your progress and growth. Procrastination is nothing but a roadblock, one that you can easily overcome by being mindful of your actions and setting clear goals. Break tasks into smaller, manageable steps, and be consistent—make it a habit to chip away at your goals every day.

Recognise and overcome self-sabotage, as it's something that we all experience at some point in our lives. It can manifest in subtle ways that make it difficult for us to perceive how we're undermining ourselves. Become aware of your thought patterns and behaviours that lead to self-sabotage, such as starting projects with a defeated mentality or continuously comparing yourself to others. Replace these limiting beliefs with affirmations that reflect the capable and powerful woman you are. You are your own best advocate, so be kind to yourself and invest in strategies that foster growth.

Develop a degree of autonomy to take charge of your own life. Setting your own goals, making your own decisions, and being accountable for your actions will lead to a sense of fulfilment and purpose. Empower yourself to make decisions not based on external pressure or expectations but on what truly resonates with your values and aspirations. By prioritising your own needs, you'll inevitably gain the confidence to reach your full potential.

To all the powerful women out there: believe in your abilities and act now, right where you are. You have the tools and knowledge to overcome any obstacles life may throw your way, from procrastination to self-sabotage. Implement these strategies in your everyday life, and you'll be unstoppable. As you develop autonomy and embrace the present moment, you'll be able to create the life you truly deserve. Remember, it all starts with taking that first step. Today is the day— start right here, right now!

5

GIVE YOURSELF A BREAK

YOU ARE DOING WELL!

*L*ife is full of challenges and distractions. The days are often filled with stress, obligations, and constant demands on time and attention. All too often, these pressures can leave you feeling exhausted, overwhelmed, and disconnected from your true self.

Remember to take a breather, pat yourself on the back, and tell yourself, "You are doing great!" I've always told myself, "You're doing great, Nekita!' You do it for others; why not yourself?

If we can encourage and uplift others, why not show the same love and support to ourselves?

Have you accomplished a task, big or small? Celebrate that moment! Each success is a powerful reminder of how far you've come. Embrace your hard work and dedication, and let it empower you for future endeavours.

Don't shy away from acknowledging your efforts, as it helps build self-confidence and shatters the limitations set by your mind. Unleash your inner power. Take a break and celebrate your success! Women around the world face challenges. Acknowledge any barriers you've faced, but understand that you've already made impressive strides. Now, let's work on breaking free from the confines of your mind, so you too can soar!

You Deserve It!

If you'd like to reflect on your achievements, here's a simple process you can follow: Find a quiet and comfortable space. Create a peaceful environment where you can focus and relax. Rest is essential to maintaining a healthy mindset and achieving greatness. Taking breaks allows you to reflect on your accomplishments and recharge your energy, making you better equipped to tackle new challenges. So go ahead and take that long-deserved break! Indulge in self-care activities, surround yourself with positivity, and let the world see the amazing woman you truly are.

~

A Warm Embrace of Self-Care

In the whirlwind of daily life, it's far too easy to lose sight of yourself amidst the chaos. It's time to take a step back and recognise the importance of self-care and balance in your life.

Self-care is crucial for our mental, emotional, and physical well-being. It represents a conscious effort to improve our quality of life, nurture our passions, and cultivate a healthy sense of self-worth. Balancing the demands of work, relationships, and personal projects can be a challenging feat, but it's essential to preserve our sanity and energy levels. Consider incorporating these practices into your self-care routine:

- **Meditation** helps to clear the mind, induce relaxation, and improve overall mental health.
- **Physical exercise** not only promotes a healthy body but also releases feel-good endorphins that can combat stress.

- **Journaling** allows you to organise your thoughts, express emotions, and capture moments of self-reflection.
- **Pampering activities**, such as a relaxing bubble bath or a massage, can provide a much-needed break and elevate your mood.
- **Cultivating a Strong Sense of Self-Worth and Empowerment** - It's crucial to boost your confidence and empower yourself. Celebrate small victories, set realistic goals, and dismantle self-doubt. Remember, you are a strong, capable individual deserving of love and kindness.

Self-care is not a luxury but a necessity to maintain a balanced lifestyle.

By addressing stress, pursuing passions, fostering self-worth, and seeking support, you'll truly begin to thrive.

So, go ahead and embrace the wondrous journey of self-care.

Take a Moment to Pause and Breathe:
Find Balance Amidst Your Daily Routine

As you navigate the endless demands and responsibilities that fill your day, it's important to pause and breathe, giving yourself a well-deserved chance to regain balance and perspective. often juggle numerous roles in the home, at work, and within their communities. Discover ways to *insert small pockets of calm* into your daily routine, nurturing your mental, emotional, and physical health.

Why Pause and Breathe?

Pausing and breathing may seem like a small, almost trivial act, but they hold tremendous power to transform lives. Here are a few notable benefits of this simple habit:

Reduced stress and anxiety:

Research shows that practicing deep, slow breathing exercises helps to slow down the heart rate, lower cortisol levels, and trigger the body's natural relaxation response. All these contribute to reducing stress levels and promoting overall feelings of calm and well-being.

Increased mental clarity:

Pausing for a moment of deep breathing allows you to refocus your thoughts, improving your cognitive function and boosting your ability to make better decisions.

Enhanced emotional balance:

Taking a simple moment to reset and become present helps control reactive emotions and impulsive decisions. It fosters emotional stability, allowing you to approach challenges and pressures with a clear and balanced perspective.

How to Pause and Breathe Amidst Your Daily Routine

Incorporate some mindful practices to create a natural pause in your busy life. Here are a few suggestions:

1. **Morning ritual:** Begin your day with a few minutes of deep-breathing exercises before reaching for your smartphone or starting your to-do list. This sets the tone for a more balanced, focused, and cantered day ahead.
2. **Mindful reminder:** Use technology to your advantage by setting reminders throughout the day to take a few deep breaths. It can be as simple as an alert every couple of hours, prompting you to momentarily disconnect from your tasks and reconnect with yourself.

3. **Movement breaks:** Schedule short movement breaks, such as stretching or light physical exercises, into your day. These breaks not only benefit your body but also encourage you to take deep breaths, boosting your energy and focus.
4. **Mindful eating:** Transform your meal times into moments of mindfulness by focusing on the flavours, textures, and sensations of the food you consume. This will help you to slow down, breathe, and savour the experience fully.

Incorporating moments of pause and focused breathing into your daily routine can significantly enhance your emotional, mental, and physical well-being. Enhance the quality of your life by embracing the power of simply pausing and breathing amidst your daily routine.

Remember: a small, mindful act can lead to mighty changes in your overall happiness and health. So, take a moment today to pause, breathe, and find balance.

~

Turn the Spotlight on You!

Hey, beautiful! How often do you take the time to remember just how amazing you are? In a world that often seems to prioritise tearing women down, it's essential for us to lift ourselves and each other up. So today, let's focus on *you*! Turn the spotlight on yourself, and let's embrace the incredible power of praise and positivity.

First, take a moment to think about all the qualities that make you uniquely wonderful. Maybe you have a knack for making people feel at ease in your presence or a fierce determination to conquer challenges. No matter what it is, take pride in everything that you bring to the table. Remember, the relationship you have with yourself is the foundation for all others in your life. By nourishing your soul with love and positivity, you're not only fostering a healthier self-image but also empowering your inner goddess to shine. So go ahead and shower yourself with that well-deserved praise!

Now, let's look at some practical ways to make self-praise and positivity part of your daily rituals:

Become Your Own cheerleader.

When you achieve a personal victory, no matter how small, celebrate it! Give yourself a high-five, do a victory dance, or simply take a moment to savour your accomplishment.

Create a Supportive Environment.

Surround yourself with positive quotes, inspiring artwork, and uplifting podcasts or music to ensure your heart and mind are in harmony with one another.

Reach Out!

Whenever you're feeling low, remember that you don't have to face it alone. Share your struggles and strengths with friends, family, or online communities that are eager to uplift and empower one another.

Be Grateful.

Each day, take some time to reflect on the things you're grateful for as well as the things you've achieved so far.

By consistently practising self-praise and positivity, you are becoming a powerful force of light, love, and strength. The journey may not always be easy, but remember that you are a warrior. And as you rise, you're paving the way for other women to rise along with you. So go ahead and permit yourself to shine. It's time to recognise and celebrate the remarkable woman you truly are.

Refresh, Recharge, and Reignite

As a woman who often juggles multiple roles and responsibilities, you have an inner power that resides within you. Focus on the key aspects of embracing a more fulfilling and empowered existence, not only for yourself but also for those around you.

Key Points to Emphasise:

- Mindful self-care and balance
- Techniques for stress relief and rejuvenation
- Reigniting your passion

Refresh: Prioritising Mindful Self-Care and Balance

Maybe you often get caught up in the daily grind, forgetting or neglecting to take time for yourself. Finding balance and dedicating time to self-care is vital to your emotional, physical, and mental well-being.

As earlier discussed, this can include activities such as meditation, reading, exercise, or simply allowing time for relaxation. Prioritising self-care allows you to regain control and perspective, helping you manage stress more effectively.

Recharge: Techniques for Stress Relief and Rejuvenation

One of the most powerful ways to recharge your energy and mental clarity is through stress relief and rejuvenation techniques. This can include exercises such as deep breathing and engaging in hobbies that bring you joy. By incorporating these techniques into your daily routine, you can see improvements in your overall mood, productivity, and mental health.

Reignite: Rediscovering Your Passions and Pursuing them with Confidence

Rediscovering your passions and pursuing them with confidence is an essential aspect of living a fulfilled life. It's crucial to identify what truly ignites your inner spark, whether it's creative pursuits, career aspirations, or personal relationships. Once you've identified your passions, take the necessary steps to pursue them with courage and enthusiasm.

Each one of us has a unique passion, something that sparks our interest and brings us enjoyment. Investing time and energy in our interests encourages self-discovery and adds purpose to our lives.

Keep Growing, Keep Glowing

Do you know the secret to growing and glowing in life? Embracing self-love, nurturing your passions, and never settling for less than you deserve are essential components of a thriving and vibrant life journey. Below are practical steps to take to grow and glow:

Unlock Your Inner Strength

You, my friend, are incredibly powerful and resilient. Life has thrown challenges at you, but you've come out shining on the other side. It's crucial to recognise and harness your inner strength, for it will propel you forward on your journey. So, take a moment to truly appreciate and acknowledge how strong and capable you are.

Nourish Your Body and Mind

A healthy body and mind are integral to personal growth, and what better way to nourish both than by practising self-care? Take time for yourself—indulge in a relaxing bath, dive into a good book, or meditate. These activities not only benefit your physical well-being but also rejuvenate your mind, fostering clear thoughts and positivity.

Cultivate Your Passions

What's brewing inside that creative spirit of yours? Is it a passion for art, business ideas, volunteer work, or travelling? Don't let those desires simmer on the back burner any longer. Embrace them! Fuelling your passions sparks excitement and happiness in your everyday life.

Experience new things, meet new people, and learn from your endeavours. No one can grow and glow alone! Building connections with like-minded individuals who share and understand your goals creates a positive environment for growth. Join clubs, workshops, or social media groups to meet new friends and mentors who'll motivate and inspire you to reach new heights. Be open to seeking guidance when needed. With a supportive network, you can face challenges with resilience and determination. Whether it's sharing a light-hearted conversation or seeking advice, a caring network can help guide us in times of need and facilitate our growth.

Stay True to Your Values

In a world that can be both demanding and noisy, it is essential to stay grounded in your values and beliefs. Knowing who you are, what you stand for, and where your priorities lie allows you to stay true to yourself. As you traverse your path, don't be afraid to say "no" if something doesn't align with your values. Honouring and respecting yourself is vital to personal growth.

Remember, never settle for less than you deserve. Be persistent in your quest for growth. Love yourself unapologetically, and keep exploring your passions and strengths.

Empowering Others: Share Your Story and Inspire Change

As you grow and glow, remember to encourage and uplift other women facing roadblocks. Share your stories and experiences of overcoming challenges, and help inspire them to embrace their inner strength and push beyond their limiting beliefs.

As you conclude this chapter, let's take a moment to remind ourselves of the phenomenal progress you've made. Give yourself a break; you are doing well! It's crucial to acknowledge your accomplishments, especially amid the hectic pace of life. So, let us help you unwind and reflect on your journey by following these simple steps, tailored especially for you as a strong and determined woman.

Find a Quiet and Comfortable Space

Set aside some time, just for yourself, in a space that brings you tranquillity and relief. Disconnect from the chaos of your daily life and cherish this moment of solitude.

Make a List

Grab a pen and paper, or open a document on your computer. Jot down your achievements, both big and small, since the beginning of your journey. This will not only provide you with a sense of accomplishment but also enable you to better visualise your progress.

You may include accomplishments from different areas of your life, such as work, education, relationships, personal growth, hobbies, and any other relevant domains.

Reflect on the Journey

As you go through the list you've just created, allow yourself to reminisce over the experiences you've had. Think about the efforts, challenges, and growth you experienced along the way. Embrace the positive emotions these memories evoke.

Celebrate and Acknowledge

As you review your list, acknowledge and celebrate each achievement. Recognise the hard work, dedication, and perseverance that went into reaching those milestones. Allow yourself to feel a sense of pride and accomplishment.

Identify Lessons Learned

Every experience holds a lesson. Think about the crucial takeaways from each accomplishment and challenge, and assess how these lessons have shaped your growth. This reflection can help guide your future endeavours.

Set New Goals!

Take advantage of this opportunity to set new goals based on what you've accomplished and what you want to achieve. Set specific, measurable, and realistic goals that align with your values and passions. Remember, taking stock of your achievements is not only about recognising what you've accomplished but also about appreciating your journey and the person you've become along the way.

The crucial message here is to embrace self-encouragement and empowerment, especially for women, who often balance numerous responsibilities and face societal pressures.

By following these steps, you'll gain a refreshed perspective on your remarkable journey thus far. Remember that the path to self-improvement is an ongoing, ever-evolving process. So, be gentle with yourself, embrace the transformation, and reflect on the power behind those simple words—"You're doing well!"—and let them transform your thoughts and actions.

It's time to embrace your greatness and unleash your potential. After all, if you don't believe in yourself, who will?

58

6

MAKE THE MOVE

IT'S YOURS TO MAKE!

$\mathcal{L}$ife often presents us with multiple opportunities, and the choices we make ultimately shape the direction it takes. Much like a game of chess, it's your turn to make a move, and the decision lies in your hands. Taking a leap and making a move is not only a bold decision, but it also holds the power to change your life. This chapter aims to help everyone, especially women, gain the courage and motivation to make moves.

Embrace the Leap—It's Your Journey to Embark On!

The moment has come for you to take that crucial step forward, as life presents you with an opportunity to grow and embrace the path laid before you. Despite the uncertainties and challenges that may lie ahead, it is critical for you to harness the strength of your faith and the wisdom gleaned from the experiences of others who have walked this path.

HOW TO FORGE AHEAD WITH CONFIDENCE AND FAITH

Trust in the Creator's Plan: Understand that God has a remarkable

59

plan for your life, even when it may seem unclear or fraught with obstacles. Embrace His guidance, trust in His wisdom, and allow Him to lead you on this path, knowing that every turn has been meticulously prepared to match your unique strengths and inherent potential.

Learning from the Experiences of Others: Throughout history, there have been countless examples of Christian women who have successfully navigated the complexities of life with grace, strength, and resilience. Drawing upon their wisdom, you can develop a growth mindset that will enable you to face the challenges of every new stage and opportunity with ease.

Build a Supportive Network: Surround yourself with people who share your values, goals, and aspirations. A supportive community can offer encouragement, guidance, and reassurance that you do not face this alone. This network can also become a valuable resource for sharing knowledge, exchanging experiences, and learning from one another. This can be a very powerful tool if used well.

Cultivate Humility and Confidence: Elevate your self-esteem by shifting your focus away from your perceived flaws and limitations and concentrating on your God-given qualities and talents.

By embracing humility and acknowledging your strengths, you allow God to work through you and achieve His purpose in your life. You allow for growth in character strength and build confidence.

Develop Mental Fortitude: In order to develop mental fortitude, resilience, or toughness, we need to cultivate certain habits, skills, and mindsets to navigate challenges, setbacks, and adversity with strength and resilience. You can develop emotional resilience and mental strength through prayer, reflection, and practice.

Factor in time for daily meditation and personal development activities that will help you foster self-awareness, self-acceptance, and an unwavering faith in God's divine plan for you.

~

Here Are Some Steps to Help You Make a Move of Your Own:

Reflect on Your Desires

The first step to personal empowerment is understanding one's aspirations and dreams, so take time to deeply understand what you want to achieve or experience. Reflect on your passions, values, and aspirations. Consider what truly excites and motivates you.

Let's explore real-life examples of Christian women who have embraced introspection to transform their decision-making process and, in doing so, have reaped the benefits of a more fulfilling and aligned existence.

Choosing a Career Path

Stephanie, an ambitious young woman, was torn between accepting a high-paying job and pursuing a career in missionary work, both of which she believed were valid expressions of her Christian faith. After much prayer, reflection, and seeking advice from mentors, she recognized her desire to create lasting change in people's lives through her professional work. By choosing a career in social work, she was able to support her family and align with her values. Inspecting her desires helped Stephanie make a more empowered decision to have a fulfilling career differing from the traditional missionary path.

Navigating Relationships

Sandra, a devoted wife and mother, struggled to balance her own passions with those of her family. Over time, she began to harbour resentment as she felt she had lost her identity. It was through self-reflection and conversations with her loved ones that Sandra discerned her strong desire for personal growth and independence. By acknowledging this yearning, she decided to enrol in a painting class, which allowed her to create her own artwork independently while nurturing her relationships. This enhanced her self-esteem and brought newfound harmony to her family.

Rediscovering Gifts and Talents

Grace, a talented musician, felt unfulfilled with her priorities and solely focused on her demanding corporate job. After contemplating her desires, she realized how much she missed expressing her faith through music. Grace decided to join her church choir and start teaching music lessons to youth members. Reflecting on her desires transformed her decision-making process and enabled her to discover a new way to share her faith while reigniting her passion for music.

Addressing Social Issues

Lena, moved by a documentary on human trafficking, felt called to address this issue. Struggled initially to find her place in the fight, but she attended conferences and connected with fellow activists. After analysing her desires, Lena recognized her unique skillset in research and communication could contribute to the cause. She launched a podcast dedicated to sharing the stories of human trafficking survivors, which not only amplified their voices but also inspired awareness and change in her community.

Visualize Success

The first step emphasizes how a clear vision of one's desired future is vital for achieving success. Imagine yourself triumphing in the crucial decisions you wish to undertake. Visualize the favourable results and the substantial influence they bring to your life. Employing visualization techniques can foster self-assurance and provide a clear direction toward your objectives.

Scripture-Based Reflections on Visualizing Success:

Proverbs 29:18 (KJV): "Where there is no vision, the people perish; but he that keepeth the law, happy is he." This verse underscores the importance of having a vision for your life. It talks about people becoming unrestrained, unable to focus, unable to reach their goals, and unable to follow their dreams. When people don't heed divine guidance, they run wild. Visualizing your success can help you stay focused on your goals and ultimately contribute to your happiness.

Habakkuk 2:2: (KJV) "And the LORD answered me, and said, Write the vision, and make it plain upon tables, that he may run that readeth it." This verse advises us to not only have a clear vision but also to write it down. By doing this, you can turn your dreams into actionable plans that are easier to achieve. Writing down goals help you to see what you are striving to achieve constantly especially if it's placed in at a focal point for daily reflection.

Identify Your Options

As you embark on your journey toward discovering new opportunities and pathways, it is important to recognize the possibilities available in your life. It is also crucial to equip yourself with the necessary information. Delve into in-depth research, utilize expert advice, and compile valuable data concerning the potential avenues to pursue. By carefully evaluating the risks and benefits tied to each alternative, you position yourself to make well-informed decisions.

· · ·

Assess Your Readiness

It is essential to consider your preparedness before embarking on a new endeavour. Evaluating your current skills, knowledge, and resources is crucial for determining if you have the necessary tools and support to make the leap. Assess your current skill set, identify necessary resources and support, and work towards bridging the gaps in your skill set.

Make a Plan

Putting a concrete plan in place is crucial for staying focused on personal growth and development. Simply put, a plan is a roadmap that lays out steps to take to reach a desired destination.

Life can often be a juggling act when balancing work, finances, family obligations, relationships, and other commitments. It's easy to become lost in the daily hustle of life without taking a step back from time to time for reflection. This is why it's important to take some time out of your schedule each week or month to review your goals and plan for the future—one that will give you purposeful direction towards what matters most.

Creating and maintaining a plan can be a daunting task. A well-thought-out plan allows you to break down your goals into smaller, achievable steps, helping to make your aspirations less daunting. When you have a clear roadmap, it can also give you a sense of direction, making it easier to stay focused and motivated along the way. Ultimately, having a plan can increase the likelihood of success, as it helps you to be intentional with your time, energy, and resources, ensuring you're working towards your goals in the most effective way possible. Thankfully, there are step-by-step strategies that women can use to make the process easier. These strategies include setting goals, identifying obstacles, creating action steps, and accountability. By using these tools and leaning on faith, women can create a personalized plan that helps them thrive and succeed on their journey.

Managing Your Fears

Overcoming fear is an essential part of personal empowerment. Fear and doubt happen when making a significant move. Challenging negative thoughts and replacing them with positive affirmations is key. Seeking support from friends, family, or a mentor can provide valuable encouragement and guidance. This is a skill that can be acquired through constant practice.

Anxiety and fear can be overwhelming and can have a significant impact on your life. It can be difficult to know how to cope with these feelings, especially when we feel like we are alone in our struggles. However, there is hope. By looking at anxiety and fear from a Christian perspective, we can gain insight into how to tackle these issues in a way that is both practical and spiritually meaningful. By understanding the Bible's teachings on anxiety and fear, we can learn how to better manage our emotions and find peace in the midst of our struggles. By relying on God's strength and grace, we can find the courage to face our fears and the hope to overcome them.

Frequently Asked Questions

Q1: What are anxiety and fear from a Christian perspective?

A1: Anxiety and fear from a Christian perspective is the recognition that our worries and fears are rooted in our lack of trust in God.

It is the understanding that God is in control and that He will provide us with the strength and courage to face our fears. It is also the belief that God will provide us with the wisdom and guidance to overcome our anxieties and fears.

Q2: *What are the signs of anxiety and fear?*

A2: The signs of anxiety and fear can vary from person to person, but some common signs include difficulty sleeping, feeling overwhelmed, difficulty concentrating, feeling irritable, and physical symptoms such as headaches, stomach aches, and muscle tension.

Q3: *What role does faith play in overcoming anxiety and fear?*

A3: Faith plays an important role in overcoming anxiety and fear. It is through faith that we can trust in God's plan and have the courage to face our fears.

Faith also provides us with the strength to persevere and hope that we can overcome our anxieties and fears.

Q4: *What are some practical strategies for coping with anxiety and fear?*

A4: Practical strategies for coping with anxiety and fear include deep breathing exercises, practising mindfulness, meditation, journaling, and engaging in physical activity.

It is also important to practice self-care and to reach out to supportive friends and family members.

Q5: *How can prayer help in overcoming anxiety and fear?*

A5: Prayer can be a powerful tool in overcoming anxiety and fear. Through prayer, we can ask God for strength and courage to face our fears. We can also ask for guidance and wisdom to help us cope with our anxieties and fears.

Prayer is a great source of hope, and belief in answered prayers is a sign of our faith rising. And that has the power to quell fear in us.

Q6: What are the benefits of seeking professional help for anxiety and fear?

A6: Seeking professional help for anxiety and fear can be beneficial in many ways. A professional can provide guidance and support in developing coping strategies and can help identify underlying causes of anxiety and fear. Professional help can also provide a safe space to process emotions and gain insight into our anxieties and fears.

~

TAKE ACTION

Taking decisive steps toward achieving one's goals is an integral part of personal development and empowerment. Once a strategy has been established, initiate the first move. Embrace the potential uncertainties and any discomfort that might accompany the transition. Remember, action serves as the driving force behind transformation; thus, it's crucial not to delay in commencing your journey.

Learn from Setbacks

Recognize that obstacles and setbacks are an inevitable aspect of any pursuit. When you face difficulties or encounter failure, seize these moments as valuable learning experiences to facilitate personal growth. Modify your strategy as required, but maintain a steadfast determination towards achieving your objectives.

RESILIENCE AND GROWTH:
EMBRACING CHALLENGES ON THE PATH TO SUCCESS

The journey to success is rarely smooth or linear. In fact, encountering setbacks and challenges along the way is quite typical. By embracing these obstacles as opportunities for learning and self-improvement, you can foster a growth mindset and build your resilience in the face of adversity. You can learn from your failure and use it as a source of feedback to enhance your performance.

Stay Motivated

Maintain a high level of motivation by acknowledging minor accomplishments throughout your journey. Treat yourself for the milestones achieved, and utilize affirmative encouragement to sustain your drive. Often in life, we face challenges that may seem insurmountable. As a woman, it is important to stay strong and motivated during these times. Here are some ideas to help you maintain a consistent positive attitude:

Remember Your Purpose

Our relationship with God reminds us that we have a divine purpose in life. The Christian woman should reaffirm her values and allow them to guide her through difficult times. Use affirmation to remind yourself constantly of who you are and how great you are.

Create Achievable Short-term Goals

Set smaller, attainable goals that will lead you to your ultimate objective. Celebrating these smaller wins will help you move forward with a sense of accomplishment. Review your goals to make them measurable.

Celebrate Your Victories

Don't forget to recognize your efforts and progress. Acknowledging and rewarding yourself for the actions you take adds to your motivation. Celebrate even the smallest of things, as that will empower and motivate you to do more.

Embrace the Journey

Remember that embarking on a new journey is not solely about accomplishing your goals but rather the transformation and development that transpire during the experience. Revel in the adventure, relish novel encounters, and acknowledge the wisdom gained.

In the end, the choice to take a step forward lies with you. Have confidence in yourself, trust in your abilities, and maintain faith that the path you choose will guide you to fresh and exhilarating prospects.

You need to understand that the journey in life can be just as significant as the destination. It is essential to embrace the beauty of your path through faith and determination. Here's how:

Trust in God's Plan

Believe that God has a plan for every step you take. Embrace your unique journey, as it is a vital part of your spiritual growth.

Learn from your Mistakes

As humans, we are prone to stumble and fall. However, the critical aspect is learning from these experiences and using them as stepping stones to success.

Seek Support from your Community

Christian brethren serve as invaluable sources of encouragement, guidance, and wisdom. Reach out to your community to share your journey and build strength through collective faith.

To wrap it up, always remember that taking charge of your decisions and embracing all that life offers is key to empowering yourself. Let your faith guide you and provide motivation to overcome challenges. What lies before you is a journey of self-discovery and unparalleled outcomes, so make the move - it's yours to make.

Seizing the chance to move forward and grow is a personal decision that only you can make. Be confident in your capabilities, trust in God's plan, and remember that you are never alone on this journey.

I am hopeful this chapter has provided you with a comprehensive guide to assertiveness, personal growth, and the unwavering conviction that you have the power to make the move and embark on a transformative journey. Learn from the wisdom shared within these pages, and let faith, courage, and inner strength propel you forward. Take this leap, knowing that it is your journey to experience, and yours alone.

7

———

MOVE AWAY FROM YOUR COMFORT ZONE

BREAK THE MOULD!

*Y*ou all probably know that saying. "If *you want to get results you've never gotten before, you have to do something you've never done before.*" So, while this saying can be debated as to its relativity and truth, the spirit behind the saying is a call to action: to face your fears, embrace your beliefs, and act upon them.

In legal contracts, we are told to look at the spirit of a contract or in a will, or, in other words, the intention of the writer while using the words he or she chooses.

Moving away from your comfort zone and breaking out can be a challenging but rewarding experience. Stepping outside of your comfort zone can help you grow as a person, develop new skills, and discover new opportunities.

EXPLORING THE PARALLELS: MOVING AWAY FROM YOUR COMFORT ZONE AND BREAKING THE MOULD

As a woman navigating a world of preconceived gender roles and societal expectations, stepping out of your comfort zone and breaking the mould can feel like a revolutionary act. But just as embracing the unknown leads to personal growth, shaking off the confinements of societal norms can pave the way for a more empowered and authentic life. This chapter offers straightforward strategies for achieving both personal and societal evolution, guiding you through the transformational journey of exploring these two parallel concepts.

In a society filled with predefined roles and expectations, moving away from your comfort zone and breaking the mould can be liberating and transformative. As women, we often face invisible barriers, both internal and external, that can hold us back from embracing our true potential. By understanding the connections between these two paths, we can embark on a journey of self-discovery and empowerment.

Understanding Comfort Zones

Your comfort zone is a psychological state where you feel safe and at ease. Though comforting, staying within this zone can lead to stagnation. It's crucial to recognize that growth only occurs when we challenge ourselves and step into the unknown. The comfort zone, as the name suggests, is a place of comfort, and most of the time it's a temporary state waiting for you to exhale and leap into your confidence. Your own fully assured state of being. Imagine you are in a war. On the firing line, there's a place of retreat to shield yourself from the line of fire. For illustrative purposes, this is the comfort zone for soldiers. They get treated, shielded, and comforted in this area before being sent out again. It's their area of comfort, but only for a while.

There are significant downsides to remaining in one's comfort zone for too long. One is that we become stagnated and eventually limit our personal and professional growth. We miss opportunities with potential for advancement and improvement, which are eventually overlooked. We experience decreased imagination, motivation, and the drive to be productive, which in turn results in a lack of new experiences and further stifles creativity and innovation. Experiencing increased anxiety over time is another by-product of remaining in our comfort zone for too long. We tend to start avoiding challenges, which in turn can lead to greater fear and anxiety when eventually faced with them. However, the benefits outweigh the downsides. We'll look at some of these benefits next.

Benefits of Moving Away from Your Comfort Zone

The benefits of venturing outside your comfort zone are boundless. Personal growth and self-discovery, new opportunities, and resilience all await those willing to push past their fears and take a leap into uncharted territory.

Here are some tips, supported by case studies, that can help you move away from your comfort zone and break out:

Discover your comfort zone: Begin by acknowledging the aspects of your life where you experience the greatest sense of ease and security. It could be related to your work, relationships, hobbies, or daily routines. Understanding where you tend to stay within your comfort zone will help you pinpoint the areas you want to challenge.

Case Study: Naomi's Story

Ruth, a Moabite widow, clung to her bereaved mother-in-law, Naomi, and set forth on an uncertain journey to Bethlehem. Ruth abandoned the comfort of her native country and its gods in favour of an uncertain future because of a steadfast love that knew no racial or geographic boundaries. Her story unfolds as a testament to the strength inherent in choosing the rugged path of faith and trust over the well-trodden byways of convenience and ease. Ruth's cultivation of both the physical fields and the fields of her own spirit exemplifies how courage intertwined with discipline can sow seeds of a destiny far greater than one could imagine, garnering not just sustenance but a revered legacy in the annals of history.

SET GOALS

Determine what you want to achieve by breaking out of your comfort zone. Set specific, measurable, achievable, relevant, and time-bound (SMART) goals.

Define what you want to achieve with these specific, measurable, and time-bound objectives. This will give you a clear direction and motivation to work towards.

Case Study: Esther's Story (Part 1)

Esther, a quintessential female role model, illustrates that with courage and clear intentions, even the most audacious goals can be within reach.

Her story unfolds in royal courts, where she sets an epochal goal to save her people. Through her tactful planning and strategic alliances, Esther reminds us that setting goals is not a passive act but an invigorating challenge that motivates action. This ancient heroine's tale transcends time, inspiring modern women to embrace goal-setting with the same fervour and faith, ensuring their dreams are not just fleeting wishes but blueprints for magnificent realities.

EMBRACE FEAR AND UNCERTAINTY

Stepping out of your comfort zone often involves facing fear and uncertainty. Understand that these feelings are natural and are often signs that you are growing.

Embrace them as opportunities for personal development and character growth. Exposure to new experiences fosters creative thinking.

Case Study: Esther's Story (Part 2)

Again, Esther's saga speaks to the core of human resilience. Her journey, woven with threads of audacity and faith, showcases a woman who, amidst the shadowy corridors of power and the palpable hum of impending peril, held fast to her convictions. It wasn't just the opulent palace walls or the whisper of silken robes that defined her; it was her courageous choice to stand in the gap for her people, even when the flames of fear licked at the edges of her heart. Her story unfolds like a masterclass in transcending trepidation, a testament to the power of an individual facing the tempest of uncertainty with a spirit unbowed and a voice unbroken. Esther's example illuminates the path for all who seek to rise above the quagmire of dread, finding strength in vulnerability and purpose in peril.

BEGIN WITH SMALL STEPS

Start by pushing yourself to try new things that challenge you. Begin with manageable challenges to build confidence. Exploring new activities, connecting with different individuals, and different cultures, and embracing challenging tasks can all contribute to personal growth and fulfilment. Gradually increasing the difficulty, will build your confidence and help you make larger leaps seem less daunting. Personal growth encourages the acquisition of new skills and self-improvement. Develop strategies to help you move further away from your comfort zone and keep growing.

Case Study: Rebekah's Story

A Biblical woman of grace and determination, Rebekah began her journey with a simple act of kindness—offering water to a weary traveller and his camels—that would ultimately pivot her towards a future woven with the threads of destiny. As she graced the springs of her homeland, her compassionate spirit caught the eye of a servant on a quest to find a wife for his master, Isaac. This encounter wasn't merely serendipitous; it was a mosaic of small steps preordained by faith. Rebekah's story illuminates the power held within everyday choices and acts of goodwill. Steadfast in her resolve, she embraced the unknown, setting forth on a path that would enshrine her in history as a matriarch in the lineage of nations. Her narrative continues to captivate readers to this day, lighting the way for all seeking to find significance in the seemingly insignificant and understand how the smallest actions can lead to a legacy that echoes through the ages.

Seek support

Surround yourself with a supportive network of mentors, friends, and peers who are like-minded individuals who encourage your growth. Share your aspirations with friends, family, or mentors who can provide guidance and hold you accountable. Their support can help you stay motivated during challenging times. "Iron sharpeneth iron, they say". Show me your friends, and I'll tell you who you are. "You are a reflection of the people you spend time with." So if these are mantras to go by, you must ensure you spend time with people you value, respect, and want to be like, whose values mirror your own or are worthy of emulation.

Case Study: The Widow of Zarephath

In the tapestry of biblical narratives, the story of a prophet's widow stands out as a testament to the power of faith and the importance of seeking support. Her tale begins in a place of despair, a mother on the brink, grappling not only with the loss of her husband but also with the impending doom of her children being taken away. Yet, in the face of such adversity, she refuses to succumb to hopelessness. Instead, she courageously reaches out to Elisha, a man of God, in a bold act of faith. With nothing left but a small jar of oil, she follows his divine instructions. Miracles unfold because of her unwavering belief and humbling request for help; her oil multiplies, and she finds herself enveloped in a community's support. This evocative story echoes through time, reminding us that even in our darkest hours, seeking support can open the door to abundance and hope.

LEARNING FROM FAILURE

Understanding that failure is a natural part of the process of stepping outside your comfort zone. See failure as a chance to gain knowledge and grow, rather than a barrier to it. I would say embrace failure and view it as a learning opportunity rather than a setback. Analyse your experiences, identify lessons learned, and apply them to future endeavours. Resilience builds adaptability and the ability to cope with change in the future.

Case Study: Mary Magdalene's Story

Mary Magdalene's story offers a profound truth: it's not the stumbles that define us but how bravely we rise—a dance of resilience that carries the melody of her legacy as an anthem for all who have faltered yet yearn to overcome.

NURTURE A MINDSET FOCUSED ON GROWTH

Embrace challenges as possibilities for growth. Believe in your ability to learn and develop new skills. Emphasize the process of growth rather than focusing solely on the outcome. New experiences provide varying viewpoints and ideas and broaden one's perspective.

Case Study: Deborah's Story

Deborah was a beacon for nurturing growth and mindset development. Among a lineage of leaders, she stood as an exemplar of wisdom and strength. With the poise of a prophetess and the authority of a judge, Deborah arose not merely to lead a nation but to champion the enduring spirit of growth in the face of adversity. She cultivated fertile ground for transformation, where thoughts did not remain static but blossomed into a dynamic pursuit of progress. Her story, which is woven into the fabric of biblical history, continues to inspire the nurturing of a growth-focused mindset, underscoring the power of determined leadership and the cultivation of potential in ourselves and others. In the echoes of her legacy, Deborah's life serves as a testament to the fruits harvested through steadfast dedication to developmental growth, even amidst trials.

CELEBRATING OUR PROGRESS

Acknowledge and celebrate your achievements, no matter how small. Recognising that each step outside your comfort zone is a victory and a testament to your personal growth. We will eventually thrive on these celebrations, which will be rewards that propel us even further in our journey.

Case Study: Miriam's Story

In the tapestry of inspirational tales, the story of Miriam weaves a pattern of celebrated progress that resonates through time. As the tambourines rose in Miriam's hands and her voice cut across the desert air, she led a chorus of liberation, marking the end of Israel's bondage in Egypt with spirited song and dance. This biblical woman's triumphant moment beside the Red Sea stands as an emblem of progress celebrated—not in quiet acknowledgement but in joyous exultation. Her story, awash with the rhythms of victory and the cadence of faith, inspires us to embrace each step forward with a spirited heart, remembering that every milestone is an opportunity for jubilation.

Miriam's legacy teaches us to acknowledge our progress, no

matter how small, with infectious joy and communal spirit, setting a precedent for how triumphs should be acknowledged: loudly, proudly, and together. At the edge of our comfort zones lies the tantalizing promise of growth and transformation, waiting for the brave-hearted to take that very first step. For countless women, breaking free from the familiar patterns that wrap around us like a security blanket can be both daunting and exhilarating. Yet, it's this daring stride forward that ignites the journey of personal growth, where each subsequent move is a declaration of strength and self-discovery. To step out is to invite a world rich with challenges that shape us, experiences that inspire us, and opportunities that beckon us to aspire more. As we unfurl the sails of our potential in the winds of change, remember that it all begins with the courage to leave the shores of our comfort zones.

For continuous learning, we need to engage in activities that will promote learning and growth, such as workshops, courses, and new hobbies. Remember, breaking out of your comfort zone is a personal journey, and everyone's path will be different. Be patient with yourself, stay committed, and enjoy the process of self-discovery and growth.

$\sim$

BREAKING THE MOULD: A RECAP

When breaking the mould our first step is identifying immediate steps we can take to move out of our comfort zone. Committing to our growth means making a commitment to our continuous personal and professional development and taking actionable and measurable steps. Utilising available resources such as books like the one you are reading now, online courses, and support groups to aid in our journey. By addressing these points, we can effectively convey the importance and benefits of moving away from the comfort zone and breaking the mould, along with practical strategies to achieve this transformation. Challenging societal norms is a significant step in creating change because it celebrates individuality and embraces authenticity. Not only do you empower yourself, but you also serve as a beacon for others seeking to do the same. In a world where women have historically been moulded by societal expectations and norms, we are now at the brink of a revolution where every woman has the opportunity to break free from the constraints that may have held her back. I encourage all women to venture out and create their own paths. Breaking the mould can be a daunting task, but with determination, the right mindset, and a supportive community, every woman can live authentically and achieve her full potential. Embrace your uniqueness, take control of your narrative, rewrite your story, and let your empowered self shine in all aspects of your life. The world is waiting for you to make a mark and hear your updated story.

8

GET SUPPORT FOR YOUR JOURNEY

SURROUND YOURSELF WITH PEOPLE MOVING
THE SAME WAY

*I*n any journey towards personal or professional growth, the company you keep can significantly influence your success. Surrounding yourself with like-minded individuals can provide motivation, support, and valuable insights. This chapter will explore the importance of finding and maintaining a supportive network, as well as how to cultivate relationships with people who share your goals and values.

Human beings are innately social creatures, thriving on connections that grow within a community, be it large or small. This inherent nature stems from our evolutionary past, where survival hinged on collaboration and forming bonds. We are compelled by this deep-rooted social instinct to seek out companionship, empathy, and support. Your tribe, they call it. As social beings, we are not called to walk alone. A 'social being' is anyone who actively engages in interpersonal relationships, contributes to their community, and draws upon shared experiences to enrich their life. With society acting as a complex web of interdependencies, our interactions give rise to cultures, economies, and political structures. Our development - emotional, intellectual, and cultural is intricately linked to the social fabric we are part of, and we, in turn, shape that fabric through our presence and participation.

In the beginning, when God created man, he gave him a woman so he wouldn't be lonely. A helpmate is what the Bible describes Eve as. Similarly, we all need to find like-minded people headed the same way we are to maximize the effectiveness of our journey.

Being a highly experienced individual, I understand the importance of personal experiences or emotions and the importance of supporting and surrounding oneself with like-minded individuals.

Collaborating and connecting with people who share similar goals and aspirations can be highly beneficial for personal growth and development. Having a supportive network can provide encouragement, accountability, and opportunities for learning and collaboration.

In my journey, I have actively sought out communities, groups, or forums to connect with individuals who are moving in the same direction as me.

You too can do this by joining professional organizations, attending relevant events or conferences, participating in online communities or social media groups, or even forming your own mastermind group with individuals who share your goals. Surrounding yourself with people who are on a similar path is empowering. It can provide inspiration, motivation, and a sense of camaraderie. Remember to actively engage in these communities, share your experiences, and learn from others. By building a network of supportive individuals, you can create a positive environment that fosters personal growth, encourages exploration, and provides a platform for mutual support and encouragement.

The importance of seeking support and connecting with like-minded individuals cannot be understated.

Human beings thrive when they have a supportive network of people who share similar goals and aspirations.

For anyone embarking on a journey or pursuing personal growth, it can be incredibly beneficial to surround yourself with individuals who are moving in the same direction.

Biblical Perspective:

Ecclesiastes 4:9–12 (NIV) reads, "*Two are better than one, because they have a good return for their labour: If either of them falls down, one can help the other up. But pity anyone who falls and has no one to help them up. Also, if two lie down together, they will keep warm. But how can one keep warm alone? Though one may be overpowered, two can defend themselves. A cord of three strands is not quickly broken.*" This verse emphasizes the importance of having support and companionship in life's journey. Whether it be a difficult project or a tough season in life, having someone by your side can make all the difference. We were designed for connection and relationships with others, and Ecclesiastes encourages us to embrace this truth. Where one person may stumble, another can offer guidance and support, and together we can achieve more than we ever could alone.

In **Acts 4:23–32**, Peter and John went back to their own people following their release from jail and they prayed and supported them. This reminds us that surrounding ourselves with like-minded individuals is essential for success. When we fill our inner circle with people who share our vision and values, we create a supportive network that helps us stay on track even when facing obstacles. These individuals help us remain accountable, motivated, and focused on our goals. By being intentional about who we allow into our lives, we can elevate ourselves to new levels of achievement. So, let Acts 4:1-3 serve as a poignant reminder to be mindful of the company we keep and to choose wisely those who we allow to influence us.

Here are a few ways you can find support and connect with like-minded people:

Join Communities Groups

Communities and groups are the tapestry of society, woven from the threads of social interaction and shared values. A community is often defined as a collection of individuals who come together based on common interests, cultures, or geographical locations, forming a network that supports, nurtures, and adds to the collective lives of its members. Whether it's a small rural village, a bustling urban neighbourhood, or an online forum, communities serve as a backdrop for social development, cultural exchange, and mutual assistance. Groups, on the other hand, are subsets within communities or stand-alone collectives, usually with more specific objectives or tighter bonds. These could range from book clubs and sports teams to advocacy groups and professional associations. Groups galvanise individuals around a particular purpose and foster a sense of belonging and identity. Together, communities and groups underscore the human need for connection and collaboration, shaping not just the social structures around us but also the individual identities within.

Look out for communities, online or offline, that align with your interests or goals. This could be professional associations, clubs, meetups, or online forums. Engaging with these communities allows you to meet people who share your passion and can provide valuable support and guidance.

Attend Events and Workshops

Attend events, workshops, conferences, or seminars related to your area of interest. These gatherings often bring together people with similar aspirations, providing an excellent opportunity to connect and learn from others.

Industry-specific conferences and workshops are invaluable, offering a chance to learn about the latest trends and technologies. Cultural and community events provide a platform to explore creative ideas, social issues, or simply to enjoy shared experiences.

Balancing your schedule to incorporate these enriching experiences can lead to personal growth and unexpected career advancements.

Seek Out Mentors

Seeking out mentors can be an exceptionally rewarding endeavour, forming an integral part of personal and professional development. A mentor, with their wealth of experience, can offer not only guidance and support but can also deliver invaluable insights that are often gleaned from years of navigating similar paths. Mentees benefit from tailored advice that can help in circumventing pitfalls and accelerating their growth trajectory.

Furthermore, mentors often provide a network of contacts, opening doors that might otherwise remain closed. By investing in these relationships, you can gain a clearer sense of direction, build your confidence, and develop strategies for long-term success that are both pragmatic and ambitious. In essence, mentors can be both catalysts and compasses, sparking progress while ensuring alignment with your broader career and life goals.

Find mentors who have already accomplished what you aspire to achieve. A mentor can offer guidance, share insights, and provide valuable support throughout your journey. Look for mentors in your professional field, personal interests, or any area you want to grow in.

Utilize Social Media and Online Platforms

In today's digital age, the influence of social media and online platforms cannot be overstated. Enterprises employ these powerful tools to expand their reach, engage with diverse audiences, and amplify brand awareness. Social media channels provide a space where brands can showcase their personalities and values, fostering a community around their products or services. Meanwhile, professional networks like LinkedIn are invaluable for B2B marketing (business-to-business marketing, which refers to the process of one business informing another business about a product or service) and industry networking, establishing thought leadership, and recruiting talent. Content creators utilise YouTube, Instagram, and TikTok to share their creativity, educate, and entertain, tapping into the zeitgeist to build followings and drive trends. For individuals, these platforms offer an avenue for personal branding, networking, and even activism, as voices rise in unison for causes that matter. The potential of social media and online presence is limitless, but success lies in strategic, authentic, and responsive use—the elements that resonate in the digital din (digital interface).

Explore social media platforms, online communities, and forums that cater to your interests. Engage in discussions, share your journey, and connect with individuals who have similar goals. Online platforms can offer a vast network of like-minded people from around the world.

Form an Accountability Group

Create or join a group of individuals who are pursuing similar goals. This could be a mastermind group, an accountability partnership, or a study group. Regularly meeting and supporting one another can provide motivation, accountability, and a sense of community.

Forming an accountability group can be a powerful strategy for achieving your goals and maintaining productivity. To start, identify individuals who share similar objectives and are committed to mutual success. Ensure that the group size is manageable, often ranging from three to five members, to facilitate meaningful interaction and support. Establish clear and common goals, and then set regular meeting times, either virtually or in person, to discuss progress, setbacks, and strategies for overcoming obstacles. For effective operation, assign roles, such as a facilitator to guide the meetings or a timekeeper to ensure discussions are concise and focused. Encourage openness and trust among members, which will foster a supportive environment where everyone feels comfortable sharing their successes and challenges. Create a system for tracking progress and holding each other accountable, whether through shared documents, regular updates, or constructive feedback sessions. With these steps, an accountability group can become a motivational powerhouse, driving all members towards personal growth and goal attainment.

Remember, building a supportive network takes time and effort. Be proactive in seeking out connections, be open to sharing your own experiences, and be willing to offer support to others as well. Surrounding yourself with like-minded individuals can help you stay motivated, exchange knowledge, and provide valuable encouragement throughout your journey.

The Importance and impact of the Support and Networks mentioned above include:

- Emotional Support: Having friends and colleagues who understand your struggles and triumphs can provide emotional relief and encouragement.
- Motivation: Being around motivated individuals can inspire you to stay committed to your goals.
- Accountability: A supportive network helps keep you accountable, ensuring you remain focused and dedicated.
- Resource Sharing: Access to collective knowledge, experiences, and resources can accelerate your progress.
- Constructive Feedback: Constructive criticism from trusted individuals can help you grow and improve.
- Identify Your Goals and Values: Clearly define what you want to achieve and the values that are important to you.
- Finding Like-Minded Individuals: helps you to be more resolute in your goals.
- Join Interest Groups and Communities: Participate in clubs, online forums, and professional associations relevant to your interests.

- Attend Networking Events: Conferences, workshops, and seminars are excellent places to meet people with similar ambitions.
- Engaging in Social Media: Using platforms like LinkedIn, Facebook groups, and Twitter to connect with individuals in your field.
- Volunteering and Collaborating: Working on projects or volunteering for causes you care about can introduce you to like-minded people.
- Cultivating Strong Relationships
- Being Genuine: Authenticity fosters trust and deeper connections.
- Offer Help and Support: Be willing to help others without expecting anything in return.
- Communicating Effectively: Maintain open and honest communication with your network.
- Showing Appreciation: Acknowledge the support and contributions of others.
- Staying Connected: Regularly check in with your network to maintain strong relationships.
- Overcoming Challenges
- Dealing with Negative Influences: Learn to recognize and distance yourself from negative or unsupportive individuals.
- Handling Conflicts: Address conflicts with empathy and seek to understand different perspectives.
- Balancing Relationships: Manage your time and energy to maintain a healthy balance between giving and receiving support.

Real-Life Examples:

Case Study 1: An entrepreneur who succeeded by joining a start-up incubator after receiving mentorship from experienced business owners.

Case Study 2: A student who improved academically by forming a study group with peers aiming for similar academic goals.

Case Study 3: An artist who gained exposure and opportunities by participating in local art communities and collaborating with fellow artists.

Action Steps:

- Reflect on Your Goals: Spend some time thinking about what you want to achieve and what kind of support you need.
- Identify Potential Networks: Make a list of groups, events, and communities that align with your interests.
- Reach Out: Take the initiative to join these groups and start building connections.
- Maintain Relationships: Regularly engage with your network and offer support where you can.
- Evaluate and Adjust: Periodically assess your support system and adjust it to ensure it continues to serve your needs.

This chapter, enriched with personal anecdotes and actionable advice, serves as a guide if you are looking to build a supportive network that will propel you towards your aspirations.

Surrounding yourself with people who are moving in the same direction as you can be a powerful catalyst for achieving your goals. By building and nurturing a supportive network, you not only enhance your own growth but also contribute positively to the journeys of others. Remember, success is often a collective effort, and the right support system can make all the difference. Embarking on a journey can be intimidating, especially if you feel alone. But the truth is, many people are on similar paths. By reaching out, we can find the support and community that we need to thrive. Whether it's a book club or a Facebook group, there's always a way to connect with like-minded individuals. The benefits of surrounding ourselves with positive, supportive people are endless. We become inspired, motivated, and energized. We have the accountability we need to stay on track and achieve our goals. So, if you're feeling stuck, remember that you're not alone. Reach out, and find your tribe.

9

———

POWER OF INFLUENCE

*I*nfluence is a subtle yet powerful force that shapes our decisions, behaviours, and ultimately our lives. Understanding and harnessing the power of influence can help you achieve your goals and positively impact those around you.

This chapter explores the various dimensions of influence, how it operates, and ways to become a more influential individual.

You influence people every day, whether you know it or not. People in your sphere of contact. You interact with both familiar and unfamiliar individuals. You encounter people at the market, in the church, and at the store. It's all the same: you have the power to influence them.

The power of influence refers to the ability to affect the thoughts, beliefs, attitudes, behaviours, or actions of others. It is the capacity to make a significant impact or inspire change in individuals or even larger groups.

Influence can be derived from various sources and can manifest in different forms.

Influence plays a significant role in various aspects of life, including personal relationships, professional interactions, leadership, and societal change. Understanding Influence

DEFINITION: Influence is the capacity to have an effect on the character, development, or behaviour of someone or something.

Types of Influence:

- *Direct Influence*: Explicit efforts to shape someone's actions through requests, instructions, or guidance.
- *Indirect Influence:* More subtle, often unintentional, effects on others through example, reputation, or environment.

The Psychology of Influence

- *Social Proof*: People tend to follow the actions of others. Demonstrating that others are already taking a desired action can encourage similar behaviour.
- *Reciprocity*: The principle that people feel obligated to return favours. Providing value first can make others more likely to support you.
- *Authority*: People are more likely to follow the lead of individuals perceived as experts or authority figures.

COMMITMENT AND CONSISTENCY

Once people commit to something, they are more likely to continue in that direction to remain consistent with their initial decision.

Liking

People are more susceptible to the influence of those they like. Building rapport and finding common ground can increase your influence.

Scarcity

Perceived scarcity can increase demand. Highlighting the unique or limited nature of an opportunity can make it more appealing.

BUILDING YOUR INFLUENCE

Establish Credibility

Demonstrate expertise and integrity in your field. Consistent, reliable performance builds trust.

Develop Relationships

Invest time in building strong, genuine connections. Relationships are the foundation of influence.

Communicate Effectively

Clear, persuasive communication is key. Tailor your message to your audience and listen actively.

Be a Role Model

Lead by example. Your actions often speak louder than words and can inspire others to follow.

Provide Value

Focus on how you can help others achieve their goals. Your influence grows when others perceive you as a valuable resource.

Leveraging Influence for Positive Change

Mentorship

Use your influence to guide and support others in their personal and professional development.

Leadership

In leadership roles, influence is crucial for motivating and aligning your team towards common objectives.

Advocacy

Influence can be a powerful tool for advocating for causes you believe in, whether in your community or on a larger scale.

Conflict Resolution

Effective influencers can mediate conflicts and help parties find mutually beneficial solutions.

OVERCOMING CHALLENGES TO INFLUENCE

Resistance to Change

People can be resistant to influence due to fear of change. Address concerns and provide reassurance.

Ethical Considerations

Ensure your influence is used ethically. Manipulative or deceitful practices can damage your reputation and relationships.

Building Influence takes Time

Developing influence is a gradual process that requires patience, persistence, and consistent effort.

Here are some key points about the power of influence:

Persuasion: Influence often involves persuading others to adopt a certain perspective, make specific decisions, or take particular actions. Effective persuasion requires understanding the needs, motivations, and values of the people you are trying to influence. It is a fundamental aspect of influence. It entails compellingly presenting arguments, ideas, or information to sway someone's opinion or decision-making. Effective persuasion often relies on effective communication skills, logical reasoning, emotional appeals, and the ability to address counterarguments.

~

Persuasion: Keys for Women

Here are a few keys to harnessing the power of persuasion to have a positive influence.

- **Identify people's needs and desires:** What are they looking for? What problems do they need to solve?
- **Understand people's values:** What principles guide their decisions and actions?
- **Recognize their objections:** What concerns or reservations might they have?

Build Credibility and Trust
People are more likely to be persuaded by someone they trust and respect. Build your credibility by:

- **Demonstrating expertise:** Share your knowledge and experience.
- **Being honest and transparent:** Always tell the truth, and be upfront about any limitations or uncertainties.
- **Showing empathy:** Listen actively and show that you genuinely care about their concerns and perspectives.

Role modelling:

Leading by example is a powerful form of influence. Observing others behaving in a certain way or achieving success may inspire individuals to emulate those actions or characteristics. Role models can influence others through their behaviour, values, and achievements, serving as sources of inspiration and motivation.

Expertise and credibility: Having specialized knowledge, skills, or experience in a particular domain can give individuals a high level of influence. When people perceive someone as an expert or trust their expertise, they are more likely to be influenced by their opinions, recommendations, or guidance. Establishing credibility through competence and integrity is crucial for wielding influence effectively.

Role Modelling: Steps to Take

We, as women, have a unique opportunity to positively shape the world around us. By serving as role models, you can inspire and empower others to reach their full potential. Here's a step-by-step guide on how you can make a significant impact through role modelling:

Lead by Example

Your actions speak louder than words. Demonstrate integrity, commitment, and resilience in everything you do. Set a standard that others can aspire to.

ACTION STEPS:

- Consistently exhibit behaviours and attitudes you wish to see in others.
- Maintain high ethical standards and be transparent in your actions.

Share Your Knowledge

Your journey is full of valuable insights that can guide others. Be open to sharing your knowledge and experiences, whether through mentoring, public speaking, or writing.

ACTION STEPS:

- Offer to mentor individuals who seek guidance in your field of expertise.
- Participate in speaking engagements or workshops to share your story.

Encourage and Support Others

Being a role model isn't just about showcasing your success; it's also about uplifting those around you. Encourage and support other women in their endeavours.

ACTION STEPS:

- Provide constructive feedback and celebrate others' achievements.
- Create a supportive environment where women feel empowered to pursue their goals.

Continuously Improve

A great role model is always evolving. Seek opportunities for personal and professional development to stay relevant and continue to inspire others.

ACTION STEPS:

- Pursue further education or certifications in your field.
- Stay updated on industry trends and best practices.

Social proof: One powerful aspect of influence is the concept of social proof. People tend to look to others for guidance on how to think, feel, or act in a given situation. When they see others behaving in a particular way or endorsing a certain idea, they are more likely to follow suit.

The principle of social proof suggests that people tend to conform to the actions and behaviours of others, especially when they perceive those actions as appropriate or desirable. When individuals see others engaging in a particular behaviour or adopting a certain belief, they may be influenced to do the same, as they view it as the norm or socially acceptable.

Social Proof: A Guide for Women

As a woman, you can leverage social proof to make a meaningful impact in both your personal and professional lives. Here's how:

Share Your Success Stories

Why It Matters

Sharing your achievements and experiences can inspire and motivate others. When you demonstrate what's possible, others are more likely to believe they can achieve similar success.

How to Do it

- **Post on Social Media:** Use platforms like LinkedIn, Instagram, or Facebook to share your accomplishments. Include details about the challenges you faced and how you overcame them.
- **Write a Blog:** Create a blog where you can delve deeper into your journey, offering insights and lessons learned.
- **Speak at Events:** Look for opportunities to speak at conferences, webinars, or local meetups. Your story can be a powerful motivator for others.

Highlight Testimonials and Reviews

Why It Matters

Testimonials and reviews from others can validate your abilities and achievements. They serve as endorsements that build trust and credibility.

How to Do It

- **Ask for Recommendations:** Request recommendations from colleagues, clients, or mentors on LinkedIn.
- **Share Client Feedback:** If you run a business, showcase positive reviews and testimonials on your website and social media.
- **Feature Success Stories:** Highlight stories from people you've helped or mentored. This not only showcases your impact but also gives others a voice.

Engage with Influencers and Thought Leaders

Why It Matters

Building relationships with influencers and thought leaders can amplify your reach and credibility. Their endorsement can serve as a powerful form of social proof.

How to Do It

- **Collaborate on Projects:** Partner with influencers on projects, articles, or events that align with your values and goals.
- **Engage on Social Media:** Comment on and share content from thought leaders in your field. Meaningful interactions can lead to valuable connections.
- **Attend Networking Events:** Participate in industry conferences and networking events to meet and build relationships with key figures.

Showcase Community and Team Achievements

Why It Matters

Highlighting the success of the communities and teams you are part of can enhance your influence.

It shows that you contribute to and uplift those around you.

How to Do It

- **Celebrate Team Wins:** Share team achievements on social media, tagging and giving credit to all involved.
- **Promote Community Initiatives:** Support and promote community projects or causes you are passionate about.

- **Host Events:** Organize events that bring people together, providing a platform for others to share their success stories.
- **Engage Authentically:** Interact with others in a sincere and meaningful way. Show genuine interest in their stories and experiences.

Emotional Appeal

Emotions play a significant role in influencing others. Appeals to emotions such as empathy, fear, happiness, or excitement can be powerful tools for influencing behaviour or decision-making. Emotionally compelling messages or stories have the potential to evoke strong reactions and motivate individuals to take action.

Emotional Appeal: A Woman's How

One effective way to make a positive impact is through emotional appeal.

This guide will walk you through the steps to harness your emotional intelligence and influence others positively.

Understand Your Emotions

Before you can influence others, it's crucial to understand your own emotions. Reflect on your feelings and what triggers them. Journaling can be a helpful tool for this. By understanding your emotional landscape, you'll be better equipped to connect with others authentically.

Cultivate Empathy

Empathy is the cornerstone of emotional appeal. It involves putting yourself in someone else's shoes and understanding their perspective. Practice active listening, ask open-ended questions, and show genuine interest in others' experiences. This will help you build strong, trust-based relationships.

Use Positive Body Language

Your body language speaks volumes. Maintain eye contact, use open gestures, and smile genuinely. These non-verbal cues can make others feel valued and understood, fostering a positive connection.

Use Positive Reinforcement

Encourage and uplift others through positive reinforcement. Compliment their efforts, celebrate their successes, and provide constructive feedback. This not only boosts their confidence but also strengthens their influence.

Appeal to a Sense of Purpose

Connect your message to a larger purpose or cause. Whether it's social justice, environmental sustainability, or community well-being, appealing to a sense of purpose can motivate others to take action and support your cause.

Be Consistent

Consistency builds trust: Ensure that your actions align with your words and maintain a consistent approach in your interactions. This reliability makes people more likely to follow your lead.

Network and Connections

The power of influence can also be amplified through social networks and connections. Influential individuals often have a wide network of contacts and connections, allowing them to disseminate their ideas, messages, or recommendations to a broader audience. Leveraging social networks can help expand the reach and impact of one's influence.

~

How to Make a Positive Influence Through Networking and Connections

Build Trust through Sincerity

People are more likely to connect with you if they feel you are genuine. Be yourself, show interest in others, and be honest about your intentions. Authenticity builds trust and leads to stronger, more meaningful connections.

Maintain Relationships

After meeting someone, follow up with a personalised message. Keep in touch by checking in periodically, sharing relevant information, or inviting them to events. Consistent communication shows that you value the relationship.

Be a Connector

When you see opportunities to connect people within your network, take the initiative. Introducing people who can benefit from knowing each other not only helps them but also positions you as a valuable resource within your network.

Evaluate Your Networking Efforts

Periodically reflect on your networking activities and their outcomes. Are you meeting your goals? Which strategies are effective, and which ones require improvement? Use this reflection to adjust your approach and continue growing your network.

Leadership Factor

Leadership inherently involves influence. Effective leaders inspire and motivate their team members, guiding them toward a common goal. They use their influence to create positive change, inspire confidence, and drive performance.

Let your leadership light shine brightly!

Leadership is not about titles or positions, but about inspiring and guiding others towards a common goal. As a woman, you have the unique opportunity to bring your strengths, perspectives, and values to the forefront, making a significant impact in your personal and professional life. Here are a few ways to do this effectively:

Develop Effective Communication Skills

- **Active Listening:** Pay close attention to what others are saying, showing empathy and understanding.
- **Clear and Concise:** Communicate your ideas and expectations clearly.

Lead by Example

- **Set Standards:** Demonstrate the behaviours and attitudes you expect from others.
- **Integrity:** Be honest and transparent in your actions. Uphold high ethical standards.
- **Resilience:** Show strength and perseverance in the face of challenges. Encourage others to stay positive and resilient.

Empower Others

- **Delegate:** Trust your team with responsibilities. Empower them to take ownership of their tasks.
- **Mentorship:** Offer guidance and support to help others grow and develop their skills.
- **Recognition:** Acknowledge and celebrate the achievements and efforts of your team members.

Inspire and Motivate

- **Vision:** Articulate a clear and compelling vision for the future.
- **Passion:** Show enthusiasm and passion for your work. Your energy can be contagious.
- **Encouragement:** Motivate others by recognising their potential and encouraging them to strive for excellence.

Expertise and Authority: Influence can stem from expertise and authority in a specific domain. When individuals are recognized as experts or possess a position of authority, their opinions and recommendations carry more weight and are more likely to influence others.

Expertise and Authority: Positive Steps

In a world where your voice and expertise matter more than ever, women have the incredible potential to drive positive change. Whether you're in a corporate setting, an entrepreneurial venture, or any other professional field, establishing yourself as an expert and authoritative figure can amplify your influence.

Here's a step-by-step guide to help you leverage your knowledge and presence for maximum impact.

Identify Your Niche and Strengths

Start by pinpointing the areas that you're genuinely passionate about and where your expertise lies. This will be the foundation upon which you'll build your authority.

- **Self-Assessment:** Reflect on your skills, experiences, and interests. What are you most knowledgeable about? What do others often seek your advice on?
- **Research:** Look into current trends and demands within your field. Identifying a niche where your expertise can provide significant value is crucial.

Continual Learning and Development

To stay ahead, continuous learning is essential. Keep expanding your knowledge base and skill set to maintain and grow your authority.

- **Courses and Certifications:** Enrol in relevant courses and obtain certifications to solidify your expertise.
- **Stay Updated:** Follow industry news, join professional groups, and read the latest research and publications.

Measure Your Impact and Adapt

Regularly assess the impact of your efforts and be willing to adapt your strategies as needed.

- **Analytics:** Use tools to measure the reach and engagement of your content.
- **Feedback:** Gather feedback from your audience to understand what resonates with them and how you can improve.
- **Continuous Improvement:** Stay flexible and be ready to pivot your approach based on your findings.

Emotional Intelligence

Understanding and empathizing with others' emotions can enhance your ability to influence. Emotional intelligence helps you connect with others, build trust, and tailor your message in a way that resonates with them.

How to be Emotionally Intelligent

Emotional Intelligence (EI) is a powerful tool that can help you navigate through both your personal and professional lives with grace and effectiveness. For women, harnessing EI can be especially impactful, fostering strong relationships, effective leadership, and a resilient mindset. Here's a guide on how to be emotionally intelligent.

Understand and Recognise Your Emotions

To influence others positively, you must first understand your own emotions. This involves:

- **Self-awareness:** Pay attention to your feelings and what triggers them. Journaling can be a useful tool to track your emotional responses over time.
- **Mindfulness:** Practice mindfulness techniques such as meditation or deep breathing exercises to stay present and aware of your emotions as they arise.

Manage Your Emotions Effectively

Once you've recognised your emotions, the next step is managing them:

- **Regulation:** Learn to manage your emotional responses, especially in high-stress situations. Techniques such as pausing before reacting and practising empathy can be very effective.

- **Positive Thinking:** Focus on cultivating a positive mindset. Replace negative thoughts with positive affirmations and seek out the silver lining in challenging situations.

Develop Empathy

Empathy is the cornerstone of Emotional Intelligence:

- **Active Listening:** Truly listen to others without interrupting. Show that you value their perspectives and emotions.
- **Understanding Others:** Try to put yourself in the other person's shoes. This helps you understand their motivations and feelings, making your interactions more compassionate and effective.

Continual Learning and Self-Improvement

Emotional Intelligence is a lifelong journey:

- **Seek Feedback:** Regularly ask for feedback from trusted peers and mentors to understand your strengths and areas for improvement.
- **Professional Development:** Engage in workshops, courses, and reading materials focused on Emotional Intelligence and related skills.
- **Self-Reflection:** Set aside time for regular self-reflection to assess your progress and adjust your strategies accordingly.

Ethical Considerations: The power of influence comes with ethical responsibilities. It is essential to use influence responsibly, considering the potential impact on others and ensuring that it aligns with ethical principles and values.

Ethical Considerations: Steps to Take

Whether you're in a leadership position, pursuing a career, or simply aiming to make a difference in your community, this guide will help you navigate the complexities of ethical decision-making and maximise your positive influence.

Understand Your Core Values

IDENTIFY WHAT MATTERS MOST TO YOU

Begin by identifying your core values. These are the principles that guide your behaviour and decision-making. Common values include honesty, integrity, compassion, and accountability.

- **Action Step:** Write down your top five values and reflect on how they influence your decisions.

Educate Yourself on Ethical Practices

STAY INFORMED

To make ethically sound decisions, you need to be informed about ethical practices and current issues.

- **Action Step:** Read books, attend workshops, and engage with thought leaders in ethics. Resources like "The Ethics Centre" and "Ethics Unwrapped" offer valuable insights.

Promote Ethical Culture

FOSTER AN ENVIRONMENT OF INTEGRITY

Encourage ethical behaviour in your community or workplace.

- **Action Step:** Create policies that promote ethical practices and provide training on ethics. Recognise and reward ethical behaviour.

Make Informed Decisions

Weigh the Consequences

Consider the short and long-term consequences of your decisions.

- **Action Step:** Use ethical decision-making models, such as the Four-Way Test (Is it the truth?) Is it fair to all concerned? Will it foster goodwill and stronger friendships? Is it beneficial for everyone involved to evaluate your choices?

Stand Up for What's Right

Speak Out Against Unethical Behaviour

Don't shy away from addressing unethical behaviour when you encounter it.

- **Action Step:** If you witness unethical practices, report them through the appropriate channels. Support initiatives and organisations that promote ethical conduct.

Advocate for Change

Drive Social Impact

Use your voice and influence to advocate for ethical practices and positive change in society.

Action Step: Get involved in advocacy and volunteer work. Support policies and initiatives that align with your ethical values.

By integrating these steps into your life, you'll not only enhance your own ethical decision-making abilities but also inspire and empower those around you to act ethically. Remember: Your influence as a woman can spark significant positive change in your community and beyond.

~

Positive Impact

Influence can act as a force for positive change. By using your influence to promote ideas, behaviours, and actions that benefit others and society as a whole, you can make a meaningful difference in the world.

Remember, influence is not about manipulation or exerting control over others. It's about effectively communicating, inspiring, and guiding others toward positive outcomes.

Developing your influencing skills requires building trust, cultivating strong relationships, and understanding the perspectives of those you seek to influence.

It's important to recognize that influence can be used positively or negatively. Ethical influence seeks to empower and inspire others for positive change, while unethical influence manipulates or exploits others for personal gain.

Understanding the responsibility that comes with influence is crucial to using it wisely and ethically.

Ultimately, the power of influence can be a force for driving positive change, inspiring others, and making a meaningful impact in various aspects of life, including personal relationships, leadership roles, social movements, and more.

The impact of your influence on others can be significant and far-reaching. When you have the power to influence others, your words, actions, and decisions can shape their thoughts, beliefs, attitudes, and behaviours.

Here are some key points regarding the impact of influence on others:

Behaviour and Actions

Influence has the power to affect people's behaviour. Whether through direct guidance, role modelling, or social pressure, individuals can be influenced to change their actions and engage in specific behaviours. This can range from personal habits and routines to more significant lifestyle changes. can directly impact the behaviour and actions of individuals. By providing guidance, setting examples, or offering persuasive arguments, you can influence others to take specific actions or make certain choices.

Decision Making

Influence can affect the decision-making process of others. Your opinions, recommendations, or expertise can sway their choices and lead them to make decisions they wouldn't have otherwise made.

Influence can significantly impact how people make decisions. When individuals are influenced by others, their choices may be shaped by external factors such as advice, opinions, or social pressures. The influence can either support informed decision-making or lead to bias and conformity.

Beliefs and Attitudes

Influence can shape the beliefs and attitudes of others. Through persuasive communication, sharing knowledge, and presenting compelling arguments, you can influence how others perceive certain ideas, issues, or concepts.

Additionally, individuals can adopt new perspectives, change their opinions, or develop new attitudes toward various topics through persuasive communication, exposure to new ideas, or social interactions.

Motivation and Inspiration

Influence can motivate and inspire others to strive for personal growth, pursue goals, or overcome challenges. Your words of encouragement, support, and belief in their abilities can have a profound impact on their self-confidence and drive.

Personal Development

Positive influence can contribute to other people's personal development. By providing guidance, sharing experiences, and offering constructive feedback, you can help individuals develop new skills, broaden their perspectives, and reach their full potential.

Relationships and Interactions

Influence can shape the dynamics of relationships and interactions. By fostering open communication, demonstrating empathy, and modelling positive behaviours, you can influence the quality and depth of relationships with others.

Empowerment and Empathy

Positively influencing others can empower them to take control of their lives, make informed choices, and realize their potential. By understanding and empathizing with their needs and aspirations, you can provide support and guidance that empowers them to grow and succeed.

It's important to approach influence with responsibility and empathy, considering the potential impact on others' well-being and autonomy. Aim to use your influence in ways that uplift, inspire, and bring about positive change, respecting the individuality and agency of those you seek to influence.

The impact of influence on others can be profound and far-reaching.

Here are some key aspects to consider regarding the impact of influence on individuals:

Personal Growth: Positive influence can inspire personal growth and development. Mentors, role models, or supportive communities can motivate individuals to improve themselves, acquire new skills, and strive for higher levels of achievement.

Relationships

Influence plays a crucial role in shaping and maintaining relationships. People can influence each other's emotions, communication patterns, and interactions. Positive influence can strengthen relationships, foster collaboration, and build trust, while negative influence can strain relationships and create conflicts.

Organizational Culture

Influence within organizations has a profound impact on the culture and dynamics of the workplace. Leaders and influential individuals can shape the values, norms, and behaviours that prevail within an organization, influencing employee engagement, productivity, and overall organizational success.

Societal Change

Influence on a broader scale can lead to significant societal change. Influential figures, movements, and ideas can inspire collective action, challenge social norms, and drive progress in areas such as civil rights, environmental conservation, or cultural shifts.

It's important to recognize the potential consequences of influence and exercise it responsibly. Being mindful of the impact we have on others allows us to strive for positive influence, promoting growth, well-being, and ethical behaviour.

Real-Life Examples:

Example 1: A business leader who transformed company culture by promoting transparency and open communication, thereby influencing employee morale and productivity.

Example 2: A community organizer who mobilized local resources and volunteers to create impactful social change.

Example 3: A teacher who inspired students to pursue higher education and personal growth through dedicated mentorship and support.

Action Steps:

- Assess Your Current Influence: Reflect on your current level of influence and identify areas for improvement.
- Build Expertise: Invest in continuous learning to enhance your knowledge and skills.
- Expand Your Network: Actively seek opportunities to connect with new people and strengthen existing relationships.
- Practice Ethical Influence: Commit to using your influence responsibly and ethically.
- Seek Feedback: Regularly ask for feedback from those you influence to understand your impact and make necessary adjustments.
- By integrating these principles and strategies into your daily life, you can harness the power of influence to

achieve your goals and make a meaningful difference in
the lives of others.

The power of influence, when understood and harnessed effectively, can lead to significant personal and professional growth. By focusing on building credibility, developing relationships, and communicating effectively, you can enhance your ability to influence others positively.

Remember, with enormous influence comes great responsibility—use it wisely to create a positive impact in your world.

THE IMPACT ON OTHERS

STARTING POINT AND FINISHING POINT

The saying "It's not where you start but where you finish" emphasises that your achievements, not your initial circumstances, determine the true measure of success. This means that what truly matters is the outcome of your efforts, rather than the conditions you began with. Regardless of our starting points, we possess the power and capability to achieve greatness.

This concept liberates us, encouraging us to focus on our destinations rather than our origins. It highlights that our initial situations do not dictate our success; instead, our actions and perseverance shape our ultimate achievements. Whether one begins in a place of privilege or faces significant challenges, this saying reminds us that our choices are what ultimately determine our fate.

Additionally, it suggests that the journey towards our goals is as crucial as the destination. The struggles and obstacles we overcome along the way prepare us for the challenges and successes at the finish line. It's a reminder to appreciate the entire process, not just the result.

Ultimately, this phrase serves as a source of inspiration and motivation, encouraging us to never give up and to keep striving towards our dreams, no matter where we begin. Whether we start at the bottom or the top, the most significant triumph comes from the effort and determination we invest along the way. Let's embark on a journey through the depths of knowledge, where we stumble upon some crucial gems worthy of attention. Here are a few key points worthy of note:

Growth and Progress

The focus is on personal growth, progress, and the journey rather than solely on the starting position. Regardless of your initial advantages or disadvantages, what truly matters is the progress you make and the distance you cover along the way.

Overcoming Challenges

Starting from a less favourable position or facing obstacles does not dictate your ultimate success. It's about the determination, resilience, and efforts you put forth to overcome challenges and move forward.

Perseverance and Resilience

The emphasis is on perseverance and resilience to keep going despite setbacks or unfavourable circumstances. It's about maintaining a positive mindset, learning from failures, and continuing to work towards your goals.

Achieving Personal Best

The goal is to strive for personal excellence and improvement, regardless of external comparisons or benchmarks. It's about reaching your potential and surpassing your expectations, rather than comparing yourself to others.

Celebrating the Journey

The emphasis is on appreciating and acknowledging the progress made throughout the journey, regardless of the outcome. Each step forward, each lesson learned, and each achievement along the way contribute to personal growth and development.

Remember, everyone's journey is unique, and success is subjective. It's important to define what success means to you personally, and to celebrate your progress and accomplishments. While the starting point may influence your circumstances, it doesn't determine your ultimate destination.

The key is to keep moving forward, remain resilient, and focus on the growth and development that occur along the way.

"It's not where you start but where you finish" is a common saying that emphasizes the importance of the result or outcome rather than the initial circumstances or starting point.

Here are a few key points to consider regarding this idea.

Progress and Growth: The saying highlights the significance of progress and growth. Regardless of where you begin, what matters most is the journey you undertake and the improvements you make along the way. It's about constantly moving forward and striving for personal and professional development.

Overcoming Challenges

Starting from a less advantageous position does not determine your final destination. It's the ability to overcome obstacles, face challenges, and persist in pursuing your goals that ultimately matters. Your resilience, determination, and ability to adapt can make a significant difference in reaching your desired outcome.

Perseverance and Resilience

The saying implies that success is often a result of perseverance and resilience. It's the willingness to keep going, even in the face of setbacks or hardships, that can lead to eventual achievement. How you respond to challenges and setbacks can significantly impact your ability to finish strong.

Learning and Adaptation

The journey toward the finish line often involves learning, growth, and adaptation. It's not just about the result but also the experiences, lessons, and skills acquired along the way. Embracing a growth mindset and being open to continuous learning can contribute to your overall success.

Redefining Success

The saying challenges the notion that success is solely defined by where you start. It encourages a broader perspective that considers personal growth, character development, and the positive impact you have on others. Success is not solely determined by external factors but also by your internal journey.

Ultimately, while your starting point can influence your initial circumstances, it doesn't have to dictate your outcome. Your effort, choices, and tenacity can help you reach your goals and finish strong, no matter where you started.

I hope that through this book, I have been able to empower you and change your mindset. In summary, it's important to have clear goals to improve your life. Take action towards achieving these goals and prioritize your physical and mental health, as they have a significant impact on your overall well-being. Surround yourself with positive individuals who provide support and encouragement. It's important to remember that you have the power to make positive changes in your life, so take action and pursue your goals without hesitation.

Please share this to encourage someone giving up around you.

Charles Lindbergh, the first man to fly a plane across the Atlantic from New York to Paris (nonstop) in 33 hours and 30 minutes, made a statement when asked by the press after the feat. He said, *"At a point, I contemplated going back, but when I checked the fuel gauge, I realized the remaining fuel could only take me across, not back, so I continued."* So, turn on your curiosity, and let's explore more insightful quotes. The last four are from me.

1. *brighter, bigger yes was right around the corner."* Arlan Hamilton

2. *"We need to accept that we won't always make the right decisions, that we'll screw up royally sometimes, understanding that failure is not the opposite of success; it's part of success."* Ariana Huffington

3. *"When everything seems to be going against you, remember that the airplane takes off against the wind, not with it."* Henry Ford

4. *"You cannot always control what goes on outside. But you can always control what goes on inside."* Wayne Dyer

5. *"We are what we repeatedly do. Excellence, then, is not an act, but a habit."* — Aristotle

6. *"Start where you are. Use what you have. Do what you can."* — Arthur Ashe

7. *"Hustle beats talent when talent doesn't hustle"* – Ross Simmonds

8. *"Failure is simply the opportunity to begin again, this time more intelligently."* Henry Ford

9. *"Our greatest glory is not in never falling, but in rising every time we fall."* — Confucius

10. *"If you change the way you look at things, the things you look at change."* - Wayne Dyer
11. *"We must reach out our hand in friendship and dignity both to those who would befriend us and those who would be our enemy."* - Arthur Ashe
12. *"It's fine to celebrate success but it is more important to heed the lessons of failure."* - Bill Gates
13. *"Everything you've ever wanted is sitting on the other side of fear."* - George Addair
14. *"The question isn't who is going to let me; it's who is going to stop me."* - Ayn Rand
15. *"Every strike brings me closer to the next home run."* - Babe Ruth
16. *"I have not failed. I've just found 10,000 ways that won't work."* - Thomas A. Edison
17. *"Don't worry about failure; you only have to be right once."* —Drew Houston
18. *"You carry the passport to your happiness."* - Diane von Furstenberg
19. *"Never let success get to your head and never let failure get to your heart."* —Drake
20. *"Ideation without execution is a delusion."* — Robin Sharma
21. *"You may have setbacks in life but learn to never quit"* - Roberts, A.
22. *"Winners never quit and quitters never win."* - Elting, L.
23. *"When the going gets tough, the tough get going."* - Vinsick, M.
24. *"Apply the lessons you've learned from your setbacks and use them as a stepping stone to relaunch and launch even further."* - Best Life.
25. *"Never listen to the naysayers. You will always have them in your life. Stay focused and keep going."* - Altucher, J.
26. *"Seize the moment. Get the help you need to straighten anything that needs to be sorted in your life or career to be on the right track."* - Robinson, S. J.

27. *"Show up for yourself, no one else will be that dedicated to your cause"*- Nekita Paul
28. *"Let the God in you show you the way "*- Nekita Paul
29. *If I had listened to limiting beliefs people were projecting on me, I would still be somewhere in the antecedent"*- Nekita Paul
30. *You are a light to the world just let yourself shine*- Nekita Paul

AFTERWORD

Congratulations on getting to the concluding chapter of *How to Empower Yourself and Get More Out of Life*! The power of self-belief is incredible, and it starts with you. Step onto the path to achieving greatness by simply believing in yourself and all that you are capable of. This journey begins with recognizing your inherent worth and potential. You may have grown up with limiting beliefs as a Christian woman, but now is the time to transcend those limitations. Change the narrative and understand that, with faith on your side, there is nothing that can hold you back. Embrace the truth that you are wonderfully made, crafted with love and greatness in mind. Don't let past insecurities or fears limit your incredible potential. Instead, unleash the power of self-belief and let it guide you to achieving amazing things. Believe in yourself and watch your dreams become reality.

Remember, starting your day with affirmations is a powerful and transformative practice for your mindset. By repeating positive statements, you can rewire your brain and turn negative self-talk into empowering thoughts. Imagine the impact of consistently replacing doubt and criticism with self-affirmation and encouragement.

These simple yet mighty words can have a ripple effect on your entire day. Not only will they boost your self-esteem and confidence, but they will also set the tone for a positive and productive mindset. Affirming your worth and abilities is a proactive step towards achieving your dreams and goals.

Let yourself fully embrace and embody these statements as if they were your reality. Allow them to sink into your subconscious mind and create new neuropathways that align with your goals and desires. Move past any resistance or scepticism and trust in the power of affirmations.

Also remember that you are in control of your thoughts, and affirmations are a practical tool for crafting a more empowering and optimistic mindset. As you continue to incorporate affirmations into your morning routine, observe the gradual and profound changes in your mental outlook. Every day, embrace the journey of growth and transformation by simply affirming your inherent worth and potential.

There is no doubt that each one of us seeks to understand our own identity. However, we often fall into the trap of letting others define who we are. This can hurt our sense of self, as it is ultimately our perception that matters. Instead of relying on external validation, take a moment to reflect on who you truly want to be. Consider your values, your beliefs, and your goals. This introspection will guide you towards a clear vision of your ideal self.

Now, the key is to align your actions and thoughts with this vision. It requires effort and dedication, but the result will be a more authentic version of yourself. Don't let the opinions of others sway you from positively shaping your self-perception. Keep asking yourself, "Who am I in Christ?" This question serves as a compass, pointing you towards your true identity as a faithful and loved child of God.

Allow your self-perception to be shaped by the unconditional love and acceptance of your faith rather than the pressures and standards of society. Embrace your unique qualities and talents, and let your identity bloom under the nurturing guidance of Christ. Your identity is not defined by others but by your own understanding of who you are and who you want to be.

This is the perfect moment to embark on your journey. Consider your current situation to be a trampoline, ready to propel you forward. Take some time to evaluate what you have and acknowledge your unique strengths. Don't underestimate the power of small steps, as they can lead you to outstanding accomplishments. Remember, every achievement starts with the simple decision to just try. So don't be afraid to take that first step; it could lead you to a path of greatness. Take advantage of this moment and let it be the catalyst for your ultimate success story. Believe in yourself and use your present circumstances as a springboard towards your dreams. It's never too late to start, but the longer you wait, the further away your goals may seem. You are empowered to shape your future, so don't let it slip through your fingers. Now is the time to begin your journey and make your dreams a reality. Embrace the challenges, trust in your abilities, and watch as you soar towards your magnificent potential.

It can be easy to point out our flaws and compare ourselves to others who seem to have it all together. But what we often forget is the importance of acknowledging our progress and celebrating our efforts.

Sometimes, it can feel like we're not moving fast enough or making significant strides towards our goals. In those moments, it's essential to give ourselves grace and remember that growth is a gradual process.

Think about it this way: a seed takes time to grow into a tree, and during that time, it goes through various stages of development. Similarly, we are constantly evolving and learning, no matter how slow our progress may seem. And as long as we're putting in the effort and taking steps towards our goals, that is something to be proud of.

So be kind to yourself, my friend. Give yourself credit for how far you've come. Celebrate every small victory along the way, because those small wins add up and eventually lead to significant accomplishments. Again, you're doing far better than you think, and your journey is unique to you. So don't compare yourself to anyone else but yourself. You are enough, and you are capable of greatness.

Step onto the action bridge and cross over from the realm of dreams to the land of reality. Let your determination and courage guide your steps towards your desires. Do not wait for someone else's permission or for the perfect moment to arrive. The power to take action and change your life is within your own hands.

Embrace the possibility of transformation as you embark on this journey of action. See it as a gateway to unlocking your potential and bringing your wildest aspirations to life. Your thoughts, plans, and dreams will remain stagnant unless you use the bridge of action to bring them into manifestation.

The decision to act lies solely with you. No one else can push you towards your goals unless you are willing to take that first step towards them. It is a journey that requires belief in yourself and a steadfast determination to see it through.

Do not let fear or self-doubt hold you back from reaching for your dreams. Instead, use them as fuel to propel yourself forward. Step onto that bridge with faith and the confidence that you are capable of achieving greatness.

Let your actions speak for your ambitions. Each step you take brings you closer to reality and further away from fantasy. With each passing day, you will become one step closer to the person you have always wanted to be, all because you chose to take that first, decisive step towards your desires.

So, do not delay any longer. The bridge of action awaits you, and on the other side, the life you have always imagined awaits you.

We emphasized in Chapter 7 that stepping out of your comfort zone can be one of the scariest things you'll ever do. It's natural to want to stay in our safe bubble, where everything feels familiar and under control. But staying in your comfort zone doesn't lead to growth. It requires challenging yourself to try new things and take risks.

The mere thought of breaking away from what we know and

entering the unknown can evoke feelings of anxiety and insecurity. But it's important to remember that these feelings are temporary. They are simply a byproduct of our brains trying to protect us from potential danger. Instead of letting fear hold you back, lean in and use it as a signal to push forward and explore new possibilities.

Breaking the mould may seem daunting, but it's often the first step towards personal development and discovering new potential. One of the best things about stepping outside your comfort zone is the realization that you are capable of far more than you ever thought possible. Each time you take a risk and challenge yourself, you are expanding your abilities and opening yourself up to new opportunities.

It's also important to reflect on the truth that growth looks different for everyone. What may be uncomfortable for one person could be a breeze for another. So, never compare your journey to someone else's. Each step you take towards growth, no matter how big or small, is a testament to your bravery and dedication to personal progress.

In the end, the saying "nothing worth having comes easy" is true when it comes to personal growth. But the rewards and sense of accomplishment that come from breaking out of your comfort zone far outweigh any fears or doubts. So, next time you feel that familiar itch for change or a desire to explore the unknown, embrace it. Challenge yourself, take risks, and see where growth can take you. The possibilities are endless, and the journey is worth it.

The company you keep can indeed have a huge impact on your progress. And that's why it's essential to carefully choose who you surround yourself with. Instead of just settling for anyone, try to find people who are not only supportive but also like-minded. These are the kinds of individuals who will inspire and encourage you to reach your goals.

Imagine being part of a community where everyone is on the same mission as you, pushing each other to become the best version of themselves. That kind of fellowship can give you the strength and motivation you need to keep going on your journey. Let's face it! The journey towards success can be tough and even lonely at times. But with the right people by your side, you can tackle any obstacle and overcome any challenge.

Think about it: isn't it comforting to know that you have a strong support system, always pushing you forward and never letting you give up? Surrounded by like-minded individuals, you have the opportunity to engage in deep discussions and learn from each other's experiences. It's like having your own advisory board, constantly providing advice and insight to help you grow.

So, if you want to make significant progress and be on the fast track to success, start paying attention to the company you keep. Surround yourself with individuals who share your ambitions, values, and drive. Not only will it make your journey more enjoyable, but it will also lead you to your desired destination faster than ever before. Do not forget that the power of community and fellowship is one of the secret weapons to achieving your dreams.

That being said, we must be mindful of our actions and how they may affect others. Our behaviour and attitudes have a ripple effect, reaching far beyond our immediate circle. Therefore, it is our duty to use our influence for the betterment of those around us.

Imagine a world where every person strives to inspire and uplift others. What a beautiful world that would be! It all starts with us, with our individual choices and actions. Choosing to lead with kindness, integrity, and faith may seem small in the grand scheme of things, but it can make a substantial impact on our community.

Think about the difference it could make if we all followed this philosophy. If we choose kindness over bitterness, integrity over deceit, and faith over doubt, there is no limit to what we can achieve. Our positive influence will spread like wildfire, igniting the hearts and minds of those around us.

Now, of course, this is not an effortless feat. We are only humans, and we all face struggles and challenges. But that is what makes this message even more crucial. When we choose to lead with love, goodness, and hope, we also inspire others to do the same. These small acts of kindness and compassion can create a domino effect, changing the trajectory of our communities.

So, let us remember our power and responsibility as influencers in this world. Let us use this influence for good, to inspire and uplift those around us. With kindness, integrity, and faith, we can make a significant difference in the lives of others.

Have you ever felt limited by your beginnings? Did you feel destined to follow in the footsteps of those who came before you? Your hometown, family, or upbringing may have influenced you. Whatever it may be, know this: Your starting point does not determine your destiny.

You have the power within you to write your own story. Your story encompasses not only your past but also your future aspirations. It is about the choices you make, the challenges you face, and the lessons you learn along the way.

Here is a final reminder: success is not defined by where you begin, but by how you finish. It's not a race against others, but a race against yourself. The true measure of success lies in the obstacles you overcome, the growth you experience, and the impact you make on the world around you. So, don't underestimate the power of your persistence and determination. Aim not just to finish, but to finish strong.

Let your story be a testament to those who feel trapped by their circumstances. Show them that they too can break free from the chains of their past and create a better future. And as you cross the finish line, smile, knowing that you have not only proved your sceptics wrong but also paved the way for others to follow. Your destiny is yours to shape, and your story is the key to unlocking its true potential. So go forth and share it with the world.

Call to Action: Are you ready to invite empowerment into your life and embark on a journey towards self-growth and self-love? Take a moment to reflect on the given principles that can help guide you on this path. Close your eyes and envision yourself embodying these practices—it's powerful! You could begin implementing them right now and see positive changes manifest in your life. Imagine what it would feel like to have a community of strong, confident, and like-minded women by your side, cheering you on as you navigate this journey. Empowerment thrives in supportive environments, and that is exactly what we strive to create. Let's join forces and lift each other up as we embark on this incredible journey towards self-discovery and self-nurture. Together, we can make a positive impact on our own lives and those around us. Therefore, let's seize this opportunity to embrace empowerment wholeheartedly. The possibilities are endless, and the results will be transformational. Are you in?

I leave you with a final quote of mine. *"I have benefited from various mentors and role models, and I intend to pass it on."* And I just did in the preceding chapters of this book. I have shared my learned lessons, knowledge, strategies, and practical experiences that will empower you for sure. I implore you to do the same, so we can change the world one woman at a time.

ABOUT THE AUTHOR

Nekita Paul is an inspiring and versatile career woman who dedicates her life to helping other women discover and achieve their true purpose through mentoring, coaching, and empowerment sessions. She is a 'Lawyerpreneur' and the CEO of The Dream Builders, a vibrant team of international business partners focused on wellness, financial freedom, and empowerment.

In addition, she is the founder and CEO of Empowering All Women (EAW), a non-profit organisation dedicated to helping women overcome limiting beliefs.

Known as 'Koach Kitah', Nekita is a life and mindset coach with a passion for mentoring, personal development, leadership, and living a purposeful and impactful life.

REFERENCES

Biblical Reference. Retrieved from https://www.biblegateway.com/passage/John 10:3-5NIV

Oxford Dictionary. Retrieved from https://languages.oup.com/google-dictionary-en/

Britannica. Retrieved from https://www.britannica.com/science/conditioning

Bible Reference. from https://www.biblegateway.com/passage/Philippians 4:3-8 NIV

Schwartz, D. (2013). *It's Not Where You Start But Where You Finish.*

Flying Magazine. (1950). Retrieved from http://books.google.ie/books

Huffington, A. (2006). *On Becoming Fearless. . .in Love, Work, and Life.* Hachette UK.

Dyer, W. W. (2019). *Happiness Is the Way.* Hay House, Inc.

Gates, B. (2016). *Bill Gates Quotes.* Createspace Independent Publishing Platform.

Rand, A. (1997). *Letters of Ayn Rand.* National Geographic Books.

Ruth, G. H., & Ruth, B. (1992). *Babe Ruth's Own Book of Baseball.* U of Nebraska Press.

Sharma, M. (2021). *Top Inspiring Thoughts of Robin Sharma.* Prabhat Prakashan.

Roberts, A. (2008). *The Hopes and Encouragements of a Woman.* Dorrance Publishing.

Elting, L. (2023). *Dream Big and Win.* John Wiley & Sons.

Vinsick, M. (2012). *The Blessings of the 23rd Psalm.* Xulon Press.

Best Life. (2008). Retrieved from http://books.google.ie/books

Altucher, J. (2017). *Reinvent Yourself.* Createspace Independent Publishing Platform.

Robinson, S. J. (2021). *I Love Jesus, But I Want to Die.* WaterBrook.

Rana, J. (2019). *Nothing Worth Having Comes Easy.*